BUDDHISM AT WORK

BUDDHISM AT WORK

Community Development, Social Empowerment and the Sarvodaya Movement

George D. Bond

Foreword by Joanna Macy

Kumarian
Press, Inc.

Buddhism at Work: Community Development, Social Empowerment and the Sarvodaya Movement

Published 2004 in the United States of America by Kumarian Press, Inc., 1294 Blue Hills Avenue, Bloomfield, CT 06002 USA.

Copyedit by Nancy Burnett, Gold Cypress Publication Services, Holden, MA
Index by Robert Swanson
Proofread by Jody El-Assadi
Production and design by Victoria Hughes Waters,
                           Hughes Publishing Services, Worcester, MA

Printed in the United States of America by Thomson-Shore, Inc. Text printed with vegetable oil-based ink.
∞ The paper used in this publication meets the minimum requirements of the American National Standard for Information Services—Permanence of paper for Printed Library Materials, ANSI Z39.48–1984.

Library of Congress Cataloging-in-Publication Data

Bond, George Doherty, 1942-
    Buddhism at work : community development, social empowerment and the Sarvodaya Movement / George D. Bond.
Includes bibliographical references and index.
    ISBN 1-56549-177-7 (cloth : alk. paper)
    ISBN 1-56549-176-9 (pbk. : alk. paper)
1. Buddhism and social problems—Sri Lanka. 2. Sarvodaya movement — Sri Lanka. 3. Lanka Jatika Sarvodaya Shramadana Sangamaya.
4. Community development—Religious aspects—Buddhism.
5. Economic development—Religious aspects—Buddhism. I. Title.
    HN40.B8B66 2003
    294.3'378'095493—dc21

2003012171

---

13 12 11 10 09 08 07 06 05 04   10 9 8 7 6 5 4 3 2 1   First Printing 2004

For Jacob and Lilly,
with the hope that
they and their generation
will be able to live in a world
of compassion and peace.

CONTENTS

FIGURES

A Note on Terminology

Most of the terminology in this book is from the Pali language, but occasionally I have used the Sanskrit forms because they may be more familiar to readers of English. In particular, I have used the Sanskrit forms Dharma and Nirvana instead of the Pali forms, Dhamma and Nibbāna, unless the Pali forms are used in quotations, titles of writings, or certain compound terms. All terms are defined where they first appear in the text and in the Glossary of Pali and Sanskrit Translations. Though many terms can be interpreted in a number of ways, I have tried to list the most commonly accepted definitions in the glossary.

FOREWORD

The state of the world at the onset of the third millennium reveals the dark side of globalized capitalism. For all its proclaimed advantages, the unconstrained drive to maximize corporate profits brings spiraling poverty and ecological devastation in its wake. Now more than ever, in all walks of life, people are questioning the core values this system embodies and promotes. Must our "bottom line" be monetary gain for the privileged few? Are we doomed to compete for a place at the top, or can other values organize our culture and serve our well-being? Every person who is concerned with such questions deserves to know the story of the Sarvodaya Shramadana Movement.

The story begins in Sri Lanka in 1958, when high-school students from Colombo were inspired by their science teacher to hold work camps in the poorest of rural areas. Digging latrines and cleaning wells with the local villagers, they found the sharing of labor *(shramadana)* to be exhilarating and productive, though they could not have imagined what would grow from that modest beginning. The science teacher, A. T. Ariyaratne guided their efforts with Gandhian principles he had studied in India, but recast the principles in terms of their culture's traditional Buddhist values, adapting Gandhi's term *sarvodaya* to mean the "awakening of all." That is how he and his colleagues soon defined development—not as Westernization or industrialization, but as people waking up together.

As the practice of shramadana spread and villagers began to awaken to *janashakti* (people's power), a grassroots movement gradually took form, eventually spreading to a hundred villages, then over a thousand, and now some fifteen thousand. By the 1970s the Sarvodaya Shramadana Movement was drawing the attention of foreign scholars and donor agencies, who recognized it as a rare example of "appropriate," people-centered development and an alternative to the capital-intensive schemes favored by the World Bank. On the Sri Lankan scene the Movement grew evermore visible, as funding from overseas enabled Sarvodaya to enlarge its headquarters, expand its paid staff, and build district centers, training schools, and demonstration farms.

It was during this period, in the mid-1970s, that I first came to Sarvodaya. I was fascinated by the role played by Buddhist teachings and Buddhist monks in its philosophy and organizing methods. Knowing I could learn a lot about using spiritual traditions to empower social change work, I returned to spend a year with the Movement as a "participant-observer," immersing myself in its activities at the village level. From that experience I wrote *Dharma and Development: Religion as Resource in the Sarvodaya Self-Help Movement*. The book focused on the guiding principles I saw at work and on the grassroots practices that embodied them. Ever since that initial immersion over twenty years ago, Sarvodaya has been a presence in my life and thought. The lessons I learned from it have stretched my notions of what is possible, and lent confidence to my own work, in the United Sates and abroad, for the emergence of a life-sustaining civilization.

Convinced that the Sarvodaya Movement is one of the great social experiments of our time, I have yearned for a more up-to-date study than mine. There were questions I wanted such a book to address. For example, Sarvodaya's relations with the Sri Lankan government, which had once been so close I had worried about co-optation, changed drastically when President Premadasa launched an all-out campaign to discredit and destroy the Movement. What changes did that bring to Sarvodaya's programs? At other times, when donor agencies substantially reduced the aid they had provided, and/or made it contingent on requirements of their own, what effect did that have on Ariyaratne's vision for the Movement? What conditions surrounded the creation of Sarvodaya's distinctive community banking and microcredit schemes? And the nineteen-year-long civil war, in what ways did that devastating conflict across ethnic and religious lines reshape Sarvodaya, and what strategies allowed it to serve the cause of peace?

This fine book by George Bond deals directly with questions such as these, bringing a wealth of research and a sensitive, respectful eye. Thanks to his work, the ongoing story of Sarvodaya is available now to readers around the world, and shows how the Movement's core values continue to influence its responses to changing circumstances.

These values, it is worth noting, are not defined in terms of one particular religious tradition; they are perceived and applied in a nonsectarian fashion. As Professor Bond takes pains to point out, Sarvodaya under Ariyaratne's guidance appeals to a universal spirituality. While informed by Buddhist teachings, the crucial importance the Movement accords to self-restraint, generosity, and loving kindness is not constrained by religious boundaries, nor is Sarvodaya's goal of freeing people from greed, hatred, and ignorance. Although as fallible as any human endeavor, Sarvodaya still holds to these aims, grounded as they are in the interdependence of all life. Sarvodaya believes that people can work together and has helped them do so. The ways it manages to keep on doing this, through the turbulence of a world in crisis, are worth our while to know.

Joanna Macy
Berkeley, California

ACKNOWLEDGMENTS

I wish to thank everyone who helped me during the process of researching and writing this book. From 1993 to autumn 2002, various organizations made numerous periods of fieldwork in Sri Lanka possible. Northwestern University granted me research leave and support for this project at several points during its development. In 1997 a Fulbright Research Fellowship enabled me to have an extended period of field research. I wish to thank Tissa Jayatileke and his staff at the United States Educational Foundation for all their help during that year. The American Institute for Sri Lanka Studies provided valuable assistance during my fieldwork in 2002.

During my field research, I experienced the generosity and hospitality of more people in Sri Lanka than I can mention here. Most notably, Dr. A. T. Ariyaratne and Neetha Ariyaratne graciously welcomed me to Sarvodaya and facilitated all aspects of my study of the Sarvodaya Movement. Many other people at Sarvodaya also assisted me in my research, in particular Dr. Vinya Ariyaratne, Captain Jeevan Ariyaratne, and Dr. Hasanthie Ariyaratne. who especially helped me during my recent field work with Sarvodaya.

I also want to thank the staff of the Parama Dhamma Chetiya Pirivena. Both the current director, the Venerable Dhammasara, and the previous head of the Pirivena, the late Venerable Mapalagama Vipulasara, were magnanimous with their hospitality and assistance. Professor P. D. Premasiri at Peradeniya University, Professor Siri Hettige at Colombo University, and Professor Asanga Tilakaratne of Vidyalankara University were all very helpful. The Venerable Walpola Piyananda, Abbot of the Dharma Vijaya Buddhist Vihara in Los Angeles, helped me with arrangements and contacts in Sri Lanka.

While completing the manuscript, I appreciated the encouragement of Krishna Sondhi at Kumarian Press. I am grateful for Joanna Macy's willingness to write the Foreword. Her excellent book, *Dharma and Development:*

Religion as Resource in the Sarvodaya Self-Help Movement, brought the Sarvodaya Movement to the attention of the West, and makes a strong case for the importance of socially engaged Buddhism.

I also thank my family, especially my wife Ethelyn, for their understanding and assistance during this project.

INTRODUCTION

A DHARMIC VISION FOR SOCIETY

The Sarvodaya Shramadana Movement represents one of the earliest expressions of what has come to be known as socially engaged Buddhism. Both the Sarvodaya vision and the Sarvodaya Movement arose in a context marked by the postcolonial Buddhist renaissance in Sri Lanka. In 1948, after more than four hundred years of colonial rule, Sri Lanka, then known as Ceylon, achieved its independence. To chart a new course in a changed world, the Sinhala Buddhists of Sri Lanka turned to their religious heritage for guidance in managing a difficult, twofold process: rediscovering their identity and responding to modernity.

The high point of this process occurred in 1956 when Buddhists in Sri Lanka celebrated the Buddha Jayanti, the twenty-five hundredth anniversary of the Buddha's entry into Nirvana. This celebration symbolized the Buddhists' liberation from centuries of Western domination and their hope to fulfill their Buddhist destiny. At the same time, the new nation elected a Prime Minister, S. W. R. D. Bandaranaike, who pledged to "restore Buddhism to its proper place" and espoused a leftist agenda of social and economic reforms. Both this Buddhist resurgence and the Sarvodaya Movement within it represented breaks with significant religious and societal assumptions. The resurgence of Buddhism broke with the assumption that stems from the Enlightenment and has been called secularization theory. Peter Berger described the view of religion that this theory fosters: "Modernization necessarily leads to a decline of religion both in society and in the minds of individuals."[1] The resurgence of Buddhism in Sri Lanka was one of the earliest of many movements around the world that rejected the assumptions of this secularization theory and insisted on the value of using religion to respond to modernity.

Although Buddhism provided the inspiration for the post-colonial resurgence in Sri Lanka, the budding Sarvodaya Movement also broke stereotypes that people had about the meaning of Buddhism. During the colonial period, the Western stereotype described Buddhism as "world denying," having its center in the monastic attempt to transcend this world. This view can be traced back to a number of Western scholars who

1

"discovered" Buddhism and introduced it to the West. Notably, Max Weber wrote that "early Buddhism of the canonical Pali text . . . was merely a status ethic, or more correctly the technology of a contemplative monkhood."[2] Weber and many scholars who followed him claimed that the Buddha's teachings focused more on disengaging, rather than engaging, with society.

Weber described early Buddhism as a radical form of "salvation striving" that gave little attention to questions about how to live in the world. Buddhists in Sri Lanka were influenced by these ideas during the colonial period, when the government and Christian missionaries tried in various ways to show that Buddhism was not relevant to modern society. Even after independence and the Buddha Jayanti, the Buddhists who sought to restore Buddhism to its proper place tended to emphasize the role of Buddhism in two ways: as a monastic and ritualistic tradition and as an important identity marker.

Sarvodaya, however, emerged with a new vision suggesting that Buddhist ideals and values were directly relevant to the lives and problems of ordinary people in society. The Sarvodaya Movement proclaimed that the Dharma teaches how to engage with the world as well as how to disengage from it. Sarvodaya did not define Buddhism as monasticism and did not agree that it represented an identity marker. Believing that Buddhist principles should be applied to social problems, Sarvodaya articulated a vision of a new social order founded on Buddhist values but inclusive of all people.

Sarvodaya's vision also was shaped by the larger context of postcolonial South Asia. At that time, Gandhian ideals represented the dominant force shaping the way people viewed the relevance of spiritual values for engaging with the world and forging a new society. The founder of the Sarvodaya Movement, Dr. A. T. Ariyaratne, was very much influenced by the ideas of Gandhi and his successors in India, such as Vinoba Bhave. Ariyaratne's vision of a Sarvodaya social order represented a blend of Gandhian and Buddhist ideals. From its Buddhist heritage Sarvodaya adopted the view that suffering represents the basic human predicament; from its Gandhian heritage it adopted the view that suffering has social and structural causes that must be addressed if liberation is to be achieved.

Although it was profoundly influenced by Gandhian ideals, Sarvodaya gave its own interpretation to these ideals and constructed a distinctive form of socially engaged Buddhism. For example, Gandhi used the Sanskrit word *sarvodaya,* the welfare of all, as the title of his Gujarati translation of Ruskin's work, *Unto this Last.* But when he borrowed the term, Ariyaratne gave it a more Buddhist definition: the awakening of all.

Sarvodaya's vision called for the awakening of individuals and communities to bring about a nonviolent revolution. Such a revolution would construct a dharmic society, from the grass roots up, to remedy the suffering caused by the legacy of colonialism and the contemporary social order. At the inception of the Sarvodaya Movement in the 1950s, Ariyaratne called for this revolution to build "a society whose value system is based on Truth, Non-violence, and Self-denial . . . a no-poverty, no-affluence society."[3] This aim represented both an interpretation of the Gandhian ideal and an application of the Buddhist Middle Way to social and economic life.

This book examines the evolution of the Sarvodaya vision and the Sarvodaya Shramadana Movement over the nearly five decades since its origins. It focuses on the past two decades in particular. Seeking to explain the nature of the Sri Lankan Sarvodaya Movement, Detlef Kantowsky asked, "Is it a social movement which tries to spread a message, or is it an extension agency which specializes in certain aspects of rural development?"[4] The answer is this: In the course of its evolution Sarvodaya has been both. Sarvodaya represents a distinctive form of socially engaged Buddhism whose vision and message of social transformation and revolution has evolved as the movement has grown by engaging in village development work. Ariyaratne said that "the aims and objectives of the movement as well as the strategies and structures it developed underwent change as it matured from one phase to another."[5]

Beginning as a student work camp movement, Sarvodaya quickly grew into a social service movement working in hundreds of villages. Its vision began with socially engaged interpretations of Buddhist values and a call for *janashakti* (people's power). As Sarvodaya continued to expand, however, it became a nongovernmental organization (NGO) dealing with rural development and focusing more on pragmatic development issues that were of importance to the nation.

In the early 1980s, Denis Goulet observed that the Sarvodaya Movement stood at a crossroads: it could either continue to be a rural development movement or it could become a national movement.[6] Several events forced Sarvodaya's leaders to choose the national and, further, the international fork in this road.

The first event was the escalation of the ethnic conflict in 1983 and the crisis it posed for the country. However, when Sarvodaya assumed a national role in response, two other significant developments followed. First, in 1989, the Sri Lankan government of President Premadasa attacked the Sarvodaya Movement. Shortly thereafter, most of Sarvodaya's foreign donors either cut off or drastically decreased their funding. These events led to a serious crisis for the Sarvodaya Movement in the midst of the larger crisis that was gripping Sri Lanka. Ariyaratne responded by declaring that Sarvodaya would simply "restart the movement." This book examines Sarvodaya's recent discourse and actions as they have attempted to do this.

Considering the Sarvodaya Movement during the period from 1983 to the present, this book finds that this process of restarting the movement represented more than a simple revisiting of earlier ideas: It signified the continuing evolution of Sarvodaya's distinctive form of socially engaged Buddhism. Sarvodaya faced its challenges by reconstructing its vision of a nonviolent revolution that would reform the nation's social and political structures. Sarvodaya responded to the war by calling for nonviolence and peace. It responded to the economic crisis by calling for a reform of the nation's economy. And it responded to the political situation by calling not only for political change but also for a new political system.

From Sarvodaya's view, all of these issues represent manifestations of the same problem: the structural violence at the root of the present social order. The solution to the problem, according to Sarvodaya, lies in the creation of a spiritual infrastructure—the awakening of all—that will serve as the basis for people's power and a Sarvodaya social order. Through its responses to these crises Sarvodaya redefined its identity, becoming more focused on revolution than development and sharply critiquing the prevailing order.

Chapter One surveys the evolution of the Sarvodaya Movement and its vision, from its origins up to the time when it reached the crossroads that Goulet noted. Examining the expansion of Sarvodaya from a student work camp movement to a large NGO, the chapter describes how Sarvodaya's vision and goals changed as it grew.

Sarvodaya's growth during this time can be divided into two periods. The first is from 1958–67, when the Movement began and grew, through the success of the shramadana camps and the articulation of its vision of engaged Buddhist awakening. The second is from 1967–82, when Sarvodaya evolved from a movement to an organization engaged in rural development in thousands of villages across the country. During the second period, when Sarvodaya worked closely with both the Sri Lankan government and foreign donors, its emphasis shifted from revolution to development issues. The Movement eventually faced a crisis of identity. Since much has been written about Sarvodaya during this period, this chapter serves as a review of the history of the Movement and the construction of its vision.

The remaining chapters and the Epilogue seek to inquire into the recent evolution of the Movement. They examine the ways in which the Movement has responded to the crises of the last two decades and how these responses have transformed the Movement. Chapter Two explores Sarvodaya's nonviolent response to the ethnic conflict and its emergence as a peace movement. Its peace campaign was one of the primary factors that thrust Sarvodaya onto the national stage in 1983. Although it might seem that advocating peace would be a natural Buddhist response to war, taking this stance actually placed Sarvodaya in opposition to the most ardent Buddhist nationalists who regarded the war as a defense of the country's dharmic heritage. As recently as March 2002, when someone detonated a bomb outside Dr. Ariyaratne's residence in Moratuwa, Sarvodaya has been under attack. But bombs and threats have never deterred Sarvodaya and it has remained steadfast in its pursuit of peace.

Chapters Three and Four examine Sarvodaya's call for a nonviolent, spiritual revolution to replace the present social, economic, and political structures with a Sarvodaya social order. In this call, Sarvodaya has sought not to build up Buddhist identity, but to establish Buddhist values as the basis for a new order.

Chapter Three explores Sarvodaya's efforts to initiate and develop the economic empowerment of the village and the nation. Stressing Buddhist ideals and a grassroots focus, Sarvodaya's economic program refutes the materialistic, open-economy model employed by the government. Sarvodaya's vision echoes the Gandhian quest for simplicity and E. F. Schumacher's dictum, "Small is beautiful." Ariyaratne notes that, whereas the Western economic models depend on the creation of desire, Sarvodaya's aim is to eliminate both desire and suffering. Summing up his engaged Buddhist critique of Western development and its effects, Ariyaratne observed, "You can organize greed and call it development, you can organize hatred and call it peace, you can organize ignorance and call it science."[7]

But Sarvodaya has endeavored to mitigate these three negative roots — greed, hatred, and delusion — by addressing the structural violence they have caused and realizing a Buddhist vision for society.

Chapter Four examines the third facet of Sarvodaya's vision of social revolution: the political empowerment of the village. This chapter analyzes Sarvodaya's shift in attitude toward the government from one of cooperation to one of criticism, charging that the government had forfeited its dharmic right to rule the country. Although Sarvodaya began with a Gandhian suspicion of the party political system, it followed a policy of pragmatic cooperation with the government and its development policies during the first three decades of Sarvodaya's existence. When Sri Lanka experienced the crises of the 1980s, however, Sarvodaya broke with the government and returned to its vision of an alternative political system.

Chapter Five examines Sarvodaya's recent interpretation of its vision as it tries to address changes taking place in the nation, world, and Movement itself. While affirming its vision of a no-poverty, no-affluence society, Sarvodaya has to contend with many forces that counter this vision. However, Sarvodaya is confident that it has developed a critical mass of supporters who have the spiritual consciousness necessary to implement the vision. Therefore, Sarvodaya has launched a campaign to realize *deshodaya,* (national awakening). Sarvodaya's leaders have identified three elements that have crucial significance for the attainment of Deshodaya: consciousness, economics, and power. Sarvodaya has already been pursuing these elements, but now the Movement seeks to implement them in an integrated manner that will achieve the goal of a civil society that expresses a Sarvodaya social order.

The Epilogue examines the relevance of Sarvodaya's vision for the global community. David Korten described the need for a new vision and the nature of an emerging global dialogue:

> "Having reached the limits of the materialistic vision of the scientific and industrial era ushered in by the Copernican revolution, we are now on the threshold of an ecological era called into being by an Ecological Revolution grounded in a more holistic view of the spiritual and material aspects of our nature. This revolution now calls to each of us to reclaim our political power and rediscover our spirituality to create societies that nurture our ability and desire to embrace the joyful experience of living to the fullest."[8]

Clearly, Sarvodaya has much to contribute to this dialogue on development and social revolution. Sarvodaya's vision is to empower exactly this kind of revolution and approach to life. In nearly fifty years of existence, the Sarvodaya Movement has explored and pioneered solutions for this global predicament. Dr. A. T. Ariyaratne has endeavored to extend Sarvodaya's engaged Buddhist path to the world. When receiving the Niwano Peace Prize in 1992, he said, "Now the time has come when science and technology on the one hand and spiritual wisdom on the other have to be synthesized on a global scale to build a nobler, more just, and more peaceful global community."[9] In the unfolding present, the new generation of leaders who are now taking the reins of the Sarvodaya Movement will have the task of fulfilling Sarvodaya's vision and offering it to the world.

CHAPTER ONE

THE ORIGIN AND EVOLUTION OF THE VISION AND THE MOVEMENT

The evolution of the Sarvodaya Movement and its vision can be divided into two periods that trace its growth from a Movement to a large NGO.

The Origin and Growth of the Sarvodaya Movement: 1958–67

The Sarvodaya Shramadana Movement had its genesis as what its founder, Dr. A. T. Ariyaratne, called "an educational experiment." Forty high-school students and twelve teachers from Nalanda College, a Buddhist secondary school in Sri Lanka's capital, Colombo, went to live and work for two weeks in Kanatoluwa, a depressed, low-caste village. The group, known as the Nalanda College Social Service League, was led by Ariyaratne. The work camp that the League formed was called a shramadana camp.[1] Shramadana means "gift of labor," and the first shramadana was that: a gift of labor from the league.

Ariyaratne, who was then a science teacher at the college, wanted his students to gain some understanding of the conditions in rural villages. When they went to Kanatoluwa, the students lived and worked with the residents, who were considered outcastes by neighboring villages. The students helped the residents dig wells, build latrines, plant gardens, repair the school, and build a place for "religious worship."[2] Building a place for worship was significant because even the clergy had previously shunned the people of Kanatoluwa.

The first shramadana camp was a great success. Students experienced a different aspect of their culture, and the project broke down barriers between the upper and lower castes. Doing manual labor alongside rural villagers changed the students' outlook, and associating, as equals, with "high-class gentlemen" from the city for the first time in their lives changed the villagers' perspectives. The neighboring villages also were affected: If the "upper-class people" from the city could work and eat with these so-called outcastes, then the outcastes could no longer be treated as inferior.

The shramadana camp attracted the attention of the politicians and the media, who came to Kanatoluwa to witness this event that challenged the social norms and prejudices of traditional society. Ariyaratne reported that Mrs. Sirimavo Bandaranaike, the Prime Minister's wife, who later succeeded her husband as Prime Minister, visited the work camp and praised the "wonderful spirit of service."[3] He noted further that "a revolution in the minds and hearts of every one of us was complete and the first experiment in selfless labour to realize the lofty ideals of a Sarvodaya society was successful."[4]

This "educational experiment" expressed the spirit of the time in Sri Lanka, a spirit of liberation and optimism about the country's future. The Shramadana Movement started in this context of Buddhist revivalism and socialism. Following Kanatoluwa, other shramadanas were organized. One of the first ones was held in a Tamil village in the Eastern Province.[5]

During the next few years, dozens of shramadana camps were held, involving thousands of volunteers. The Shramadana Movement expanded rapidly, soon outgrowing the bounds of Nalanda College, as students and adults from other schools and other parts of the country organized shramadanas. It was during this period that Ariyaratne and other early Sarvodaya leaders, such as M. W. Karunananda, the principal of Nalanda College, began to develop the philosophy of the Sarvodaya Shramadana Movement. Drawing on their experiences in the villages, they reflected on the goals and methods that should be used to build what they were starting to call a "Sarvodaya society."

From this beginning, the Sarvodaya Shramadana Movement constructed its distinctive form of socially engaged Buddhism from three strands: Gandhian ideals, Buddhist philosophy, and ecumenical spirituality.

Gandhian Ideals[6]

The Gandhian influence is evident from the name Sarvodaya. Mahatma Gandhi used this Sanskrit term, meaning "the welfare of all," as the title of his Gujarati translation of John Ruskin's work, *Unto This Last*. Ariyaratne studied Gandhi's ideas and worked with Gandhi's successor, Vinoba Bhave, in India. Ariyaratne has said that he did not borrow or import the Indian Sarvodaya ideas when he was beginning his Sri Lankan movement. To a large extent this is true, because the distinctive culture and problems of Sri Lanka required distinctive approaches. Nevertheless, there can be no doubt that the Gandhian movement inspired and influenced Sarvodaya in Sri Lanka. A close associate of

Ariyaratne's described the early days of the Sri Lankan movement: "In public meetings the pictures and sayings of Gandhi and Vinoba were given prominence and in study classes it was their thought that provided the much needed inspiration for the young Sarvodayans."[7]

The Indian Sarvodaya movement influenced the fundamental orientation and outlook of Sarvodaya in Sri Lanka in at least three important ways. First, the Gandhian example of selfless service for humanity as the highest form of religious practice lies at the heart of the Sarvodaya Movement. When Gandhi formulated this idea, India was attempting to revive Hinduism and liberate India. In this process it was facing some of the same problems as the Buddhists in Sri Lanka. Gandhi's view presupposed a belief in the unity of humanity and the need for religion to address human need. Gandhi said, "God demands nothing less than self-surrender as the price for the only real freedom that is worth having. And when a man thus loses himself, he immediately finds himself in the service of God's creation."[8]

Second, Gandhi and his movement used the term Sarvodaya to refer to a new, nonviolent, socioeconomic order. Working for this new social order was the highest form of religious vocation. "The spiritual law," Gandhi said, "expresses itself only through the ordinary activities of life. It thus affects the economic, the social, and the political."[9] Vinoba Bhave spoke of trying to bring about a three-fold revolution. "Firstly, I want to change people's hearts. Secondly, I want to create a change in their lives. Thirdly, I want to change the social structure."[10]

The third influence came through the Gandhian movement's emphasis on the village as the heart of this new social-economic-religious order. Gandhi opposed industrialization, materialism, and the drive for wealth. The peaceful life of the village, with its basic Hindu values, rather than the industrialized city became the ideal for Gandhi. He began his Constructive Program as a way to increase the autonomy of the village by empowering the people. This program included various social reforms, such as "the removal of untouchability, introduction of prohibition, promotion of village industries, improvement of village sanitation, . . . improvement of the condition of women, . . . [and] working towards economic equality."[11] In his campaign for *khadi*, (homespun cloth), Gandhi became one of the pioneers of appropriate technology. He said that the spinning wheels he encouraged people to use in order to become self-sufficient stood for "simple living and high thinking." Although the Sri Lankan Sarvodaya Movement may not have replicated all of the items in the Constructive Program, that program influenced and shaped the Sri Lankan Sarvodaya Movement's orientation and many of its programs in general.

The Sri Lankan Sarvodaya adopted the Gandhian values of truth, nonviolence, and self-denial as central principles for its philosophy. Gandhi believed, Kantowsky notes, that "only when an equal share has been given 'unto this last,' is a nonviolent social order *(ahiṃsā)* possible; only in such a society can Truth *(satya)* and Self-Realization *(swaraj)* grow."[12] These values were evident in the first shramadana camps and influenced Sarvodaya as it constructed the Movement. As we shall see, during the most recent and difficult period of the Movement's history, Ariyaratne returned to Gandhian values in his call for a new village revolution.

Buddhist Philosophical Influences

Ariyaratne said, "The philosophy that influenced us most in evolving our Sarvodaya concept in Sri Lanka (Ceylon) was Lord Buddha's teaching."[13] This influence is manifest in the interpretation that Ariyaratne gave to the Gandhian concept of Sarvodaya. Instead of using Gandhi's definition, the welfare of all, or the uplift of all, Ariyaratne gave the term a Buddhist rendering: the awakening of all. This definition placed the Buddhist spiritual goal at the center of the Movement; it declared that this Movement sought the welfare of the people and the awakening and liberation of individuals and society. As Joanna Macy noted, "the transformation of personality— the 'building of a new person'— is presented as the chief aim of the Movement. Ariyaratne consistently stresses this, declaring that 'the chief objective of Sarvodaya is personality awakening'— that is, 'with the effort of the individual as well as with help from others, to improve oneself to the highest level of well-being.'"[14] Sarvodaya employs Buddhist ideals to define the nature of the human potential that all persons are encouraged to awaken and actualize.

Since the Sarvodaya Movement arose during the Buddhist euphoria and renaissance following the Buddha Jayanti, it was natural that it should reflect the Buddhist spirit of the times. One figure who expressed that spirit and inspired the Sarvodaya Movement was Anagārika Dharmapāla, the patriarch of the Buddhist revival and the charismatic advocate of Sinhala Buddhist independence. Dharmapāla, who worked for the restoration of Buddhism in Sri Lanka and India during the late nineteenth and early twentieth centuries, was a living sermon on this-worldly asceticism. In order to reform Buddhism, he adopted the role of an anagārika, (homeless one). Since an anagārika was neither a monk nor a layman, this status enabled Dharmapāla to pursue the religious life and be active in the world without having the restrictions of the monastic life.

Although few Buddhists after Dharmapāla took up the role of an anagārika, Dharmapāla's life and preaching established for all later Buddhist reformers the importance of worldly activity. He described Buddhism as a "Gospel of Activity" preached by the Buddha, who "was engaged in doing good in the world of gods and men for twenty-two hours each day." Dharmapāla proclaimed that "Greater than the bliss of sweet Nirvana is the life of moral activity."[15]

Advocating a Buddhism of activity and service, Dharmapāla was undoubtedly responding to the Western and Christian criticism of Buddhism as too other-worldly. The British officials and Christian missionaries had promoted this idea from the outset of colonial rule in Sri Lanka and had used it as an argument for promoting Christianity and Christian schools. Since Christianity was identified with Western culture and knowledge, the British praised it as progressive and condemned Buddhism as backward.

Buddhism came to be regarded by the Westerners as well as many Sinhalese as a religion that lacked a social ethic. To counter this argument, Dharmapāla wrote extensively about the emphasis that early Buddhism placed on a social ethic. "To build a rest house for the public good, to build a bridge, . . . to help the poor, to take care of parents and holy men, . . . to establish free hospitals . . . all these are productive of good karma."[16] Yet, he criticized the Buddhism of his day, saying that "The bhikkhus [monks] are indolent, they have lost the spirit of heroism and altruism of their ancient examples."[17] In words that were to be echoed by Sarvodaya, Dharmapāla wrote, "The ideal of the Buddhist faith consists in realizing through spiritual experience and moral acts, the continuity of life in man and nature and the fellowship of all beings."[18]

Dharmapāla's central message, which profoundly influenced later Buddhist reformers including Dr. Ariyaratne, was that the Sinhalese should return to the Dharma in order to solve the dual dilemma of identity and responsiveness: how to rediscover their identity and respond to the modern context. Reestablishing Buddhism and Buddhist values would enable the Sinhalese to reestablish the glorious civilization of Buddhist antiquity, where "free from foreign influences, . . . with the word of the Buddha as their guiding light" the Sinhalese people enjoyed happiness and prosperity.[19]

In response to both Dharmapāla's preaching and the missionaries' criticism that Buddhism lacked a social ethic and concern, some Buddhist organizations began social service agencies. The All Ceylon Buddhist Congress and the Young Men's Buddhist Association, for example, established orphanages, hospitals, and homes for the elderly. It was not until the Sarvodaya Movement emerged, however, that social service was given a distinctively Buddhist rationale and organized to achieve Buddhist objectives. Ariyaratne has explicitly said that his movement was inspired by Dharmapāla, and that "we follow in his footsteps."[20]

In 1961, Ariyaratne and the participants in the new movement conducted a shramadana camp in Anuradhapura and worked to restore the ancient city. During this camp, they held a meeting under the sacred Bo tree and adopted a resolution officially accepting "Sarvodaya" as the name of the new movement. They also signed a resolution pledging to further "the cause of the movement in the service of the spiritual and economic regeneration of Sri Lanka according to Buddhist values and principles."[21] Given the setting in which the Movement began, there can be no doubt that its origins represented a manifestation of what Kantowsky describes as "the Buddhist renaissance which began about a century ago as a protest against western colonial and spiritual dominance."[22]

Some observers have argued that the early Sarvodaya Movement represented an expression of the Buddhist nationalism of the time, and that it reflected the values of the urban bourgeoisie, who were the main actors in the Buddhist renaissance.[23] Although Sarvodaya certainly began in this context and its discourse occasionally seems to reflect this nationalism, the Movement was, from the beginning, focused on Buddhist values rather than Buddhist identity. Sarvodaya presents a reformist interpretation of Buddhism, and attempts to provide an alternative vision that would counter the effects of colonial and post-colonial forces and policies on Sri Lankan society, its poorest villagers in particular. Kantowsky explained that "in reaction against . . . Eurocentric definitions of their countries' situation, intellectuals in India and Ceylon initiated reform movements which have culminated in Sarvodaya as a peculiar form of inner-worldly asceticism, which leads the devoted Hindu or Buddhist right into the problem areas of his own society and not out of them."[24]

Sarvodaya began with a vision of how Buddhist values offered the best hope for redressing the wrongs caused by years of Western colonial policies and for responding to the modern age with its new problems. Describing Sarvodaya's affirmation of Buddhist ideals, Ariyaratne said that the Movement accepted "a fundamental philosophy which is more in conformity with our noble heritage, which is essential to the present day when mankind has to be saved from the destruction that arises from scientific knowledge without the knowledge of righteousness, and which is appropriate to the peaceful human society of tomorrow."[25]

Ecumenical Spirituality

The third factor that influenced the vision of Sarvodaya is what can be regarded as either a Victorian or New Age spirituality that emphasizes an underlying spiritual unity of all religions. Ariyaratne wrote, "What is most important to us in religion is not its historical, political, or ritualistic aspects. These are all secondary for Sarvodaya. What is most important is the essence of religion, which is spirituality . . . Whatever one may call it, cosmic consciousness, or universal mindfulness. . . ."[26] He also talked about "universally just spiritual laws" that transcend the historic religions.[27] This kind of ecumenical spirituality in the Sarvodaya Movement actually represents another link to the Gandhian heritage, for both Gandhi and Vinoba Bhave regarded all religions as equal paths to God and liberation.[28]

Followers of the various religions might debate with Ariyaratne (and with Gandhi and Vinoba Bhave as well) about the degree of spiritual unity between religions, and whether this emphasis on unity obscures significant differences. Nevertheless, ecumenical spirituality and spiritual consciousness constitute basic premises of Sarvodaya's vision and Ariyaratne's personal faith.

The assumption of an underlying spiritual unity tempers Sarvodaya's use of Buddhist philosophy, for Ariyaratne believes that the Buddhist concepts represent universal values. As he has said, "Lovingkindness is lovingkindness. Compassion is compassion. . . . As soon as we apply such qualifying terms as Buddhist, Hindu, Islamic, Christian, etc. to these qualities they cease to have any meaning. All that happens thereby is that the spiritual quality is lost and a religious label is given protection."[29] Responding to an interviewer who asked about his view of what Ariyaratne calls "Buddhist ecumenism," Ariyaratne replied, "I know I will be misunderstood, but I mean Buddhist culture without labels. By this I mean the acceptance in Buddhism of processes, not events or persons, and of realities as against labels."[30]

Just as all religions have an underlying spiritual unity, so all people have an underlying spiritual consciousness, according to Sarvodaya. Sarvodaya seeks to awaken this spiritual consciousness in order to build a spiritual infrastructure that will lead to a Sarvodaya social order.

Following this principle of spiritual unity, Sarvodaya embraces religious pluralism and Buddhist ecumenism. This assumption of spiritual unity sets Sarvodaya apart from Sinhala Buddhist nationalism, which emphasizes Buddhist exclusivism and Buddhist privilege. Sarvodaya seeks to be inclusive and encourages its members to transcend religious differences and unite with all people. As Macy wrote, "That the move-

ment's religious identification is not exclusively Buddhist is evident in
its activities among other religious communities, in its inclusion of
Christian, Hindu, and Muslim symbols and rituals, . . . [and] in the
work of Hindu and Christian priests and Muslim imams in its local
programs. . . .[31]

From the first shramadana camp in Kanatoluwa, Sarvodaya has endeavored to break down barriers and include all people in building a new society that provides a better life for all. It has followed Gandhi's admonition
to "leave no one behind." Sarvodaya has continued this inclusiveness down
to the present.

Sarvodaya's Vision of a New Social Order

During its first decade, Sarvodaya drew on all three strands to construct its vision of a new social order. This process of envisioning the
order addressed both the need and the spirit of the time: the need to
respond to the long oppression of colonialism that was just ending and
the spirit of optimism in facing the new challenges of modernity. Central to Sarvodaya's vision were the Gandhian ideals of self-realization
and social liberation through this-worldly asceticism. While accepting
these Gandhian ideals, the Sri Lankan Sarvodaya Movement also drew
on Buddhist teachings and values to define the means and ends of the
liberation process. In this way, Sarvodaya constructed its distinctive,
socially engaged Buddhist vision of a new social order. Explaining the
difference between the Gandhian Sarvodaya based on Hindu ideas and
the Sri Lankan Buddhist Sarvodaya, Kantowsky observed that, "Gandhi tried to realize his true Self through dedication to the Service of All;
Sarvodaya workers in Sri Lanka express their Non-Self by Sharing with
All."[32]

Sarvodaya's vision begins with a reinterpretation of the Four Noble
Truths to provide an explanation of suffering and its dimensions in contemporary society. In Sarvodaya's engaged Buddhist interpretation, suffering has both individual and social or structural dimensions and
causes: It stems from individual *tanhā* (desire) and collective greed,
materialism, and consumerism. The solution to these dual levels of suffering lies in the dual levels of awakening that Sarvodaya seeks to facilitate: the awakening of the individual with and through the awakening
of society. From Sarvodaya's perspective, the notion of dual awakening
provides a Buddhist explanation of Gandhi's ideal of this-worldly asceticism, and demonstrates how the awakening of the individual is tied to
the awakening of society.

Ariyaratne described the ideal in this way,

> "Sarvodaya points to a twofold liberation objective every indi-
> vidual should strive for. First, within one's own mind . . . there
> are certain defilements one has to recognize and strive to
> cleanse. Second, one has to recognize that there are unjust and
> immoral socioeconomic chains which keep the vast majority of
> people enslaved. . . . Thus a dual revolution pertaining to an
> individual's mental make-up and to the social environment in
> which he lives is kept foremost in the Sarvodaya Shramadana
> Movement worker's mind and behaviour."[33]

Ariyaratne also observed that these two forms of liberation are interdependent: "I cannot awaken myself unless I help awaken others. Others
cannot awaken unless I do."[34] The concept of a dual awakening stands at
the center of Sarvodaya's engaged Buddhist discourse about a spiritual revolution that will bring about a new social order.

The Awakening of the Individual

Sarvodaya calls the awakening of the individual "personality awakening"
or "personality development." In the spirit of the Buddhist revival, Ariyaratne wrote that "every human being has the potential to attain
supreme enlightenment."[35] Because of the present condition of both individuals and society, however, the kind of personality awakening that the
average person can achieve in this life is far below the level of supreme
enlightenment. Nevertheless it represents a start on the gradual path
toward enlightenment, the "ultimate goal of Buddhism." Therefore, Sarvodaya teaches that before people can awaken to the supreme, supramundane dimension of truth, they must awaken to the mundane
dimensions of truth that surround them in society. Before people can see
the supramundane meaning of the Four Noble Truths, for example, they
must see the mundane meaning of these truths.

To illustrate this idea, Sarvodaya has given the Four Noble Truths social
interpretations. The First Noble Truth *dukkha* (suffering or unsatisfactoriness),
is translated as "There is a decadent village." This concrete form of suffering
becomes the focus of mundane awakening. Villagers should recognize problems such as poverty, disease, oppression, and disunity in their environment.

The Second Noble Truth, *samudaya* (the origin of suffering), now signifies that the decadent condition of the village has one or more causes. Sarvodaya teaches that the causes lie in factors such as egoism, competition,
ignorance, and disunity.

The Third Noble Truth, *nirodha* (cessation), understood in traditional Buddhism as an indicator of Nirvana, acknowledges that the villagers' suffering can cease. The means to ending suffering lies in the Fourth Noble Truth, the Noble Eightfold Path. Macy offers an excellent example of the mundane explication of the Noble Eightfold Path when she cites a Sarvodaya teacher's explanation of *sati* (Right Mindfulness). "Right Mindfulness—that means stay open and alert to the needs of the village. . . . Look to see what is needed—latrines, water, road. . . ."[36]

If people can awaken to the mundane truths about the conditions around them, then, realizing the need for change, they can work in society for spiritual and social liberation. As society is changed, the individual is changed. One who addresses mundane problems with compassion finds the mundane world becoming more compassionate. And, in a more compassionate world, it is easier to develop wisdom. Ariyaratne explained the interconnectedness of dual liberation when he said, "the struggle for external liberation is a struggle for inner liberation from greed, hatred, and ignorance at the same time."[37]

The Awakening of Society

Sarvodaya spells out the interdependent nature of awakening and development by specifying six levels of human awakening: personality awakening; family awakening; village/community awakening; urban awakening; national awakening; and global awakening. Sarvodaya's view of societal awakening on these levels constitutes a revolutionary reinterpretation of social and economic development. For Sarvodaya, development is an integrated process involving six elements that reinforce each other to bring about the best society. In this process, the reform of a society's social, political, and economic elements should take place as the society reasserts its moral, cultural, and spiritual elements. Such development leads to a society built on spiritual and traditional values, where people can live together in harmony and individuals can have an opportunity to awaken their personalities to the fullest.

Sarvodaya's ideal of an integrated development supported by spiritual values critiques the materialistic, capitalistic model of development that has been dominant in Sri Lanka since the colonial period. Opposing the kinds of materialistic development schemes that the government and international agencies have brought about in Sri Lanka, Ariyaratne said, "In production-centered societies the total perspective of human personality and sustainable relationships between man and nature is lost sight of. . . . The higher ideals of human personality and social values are disregarded."[38]

Basic Human Needs

Sarvodaya summarized its ideal of a new social order by calling for a no-poverty, no-affluence society. To explain this ideal further, Sarvodaya turned to the idea of basic human needs, which had been proposed by various international development planners. The proposal had as its center-piece a list of the fundamental requirements for an adequate standard of living.[39] Sarvodaya devised its own list of ten basic human needs, as seen from the perspective of Gandhian and Buddhist values.

1. A clean environment
2. A clean and adequate water supply
3. Minimum clothing requirements
4. A balanced diet
5. Simple housing
6. Basic health care
7. Simple communication facilities
8. Minimum energy requirements
9. Total and continuing education for all
10. Cultural and spiritual needs[40]

Sarvodaya's list resonates with Gandhi's teaching that, "the essence of what I have said is that man should rest content with what are his real needs and become self-sufficient."[41] The list also reflects Buddhist teachings about living simply and overcoming desires.

Sarvodaya's Buddhist and spiritual influences are evident in the list from its inclusion of standard items such as food, clothing, and housing, and other more distinctive items such as a clean and beautiful environment and cultural and spiritual development. Sarvodaya intentionally excluded income generation and employment, because these "needs" are tied too closely to the materialistic social order that Sarvodaya is rejecting. Kantowsky noted that, "these central categories of modern economics are assumed to have limited relevance, if any at all, for a village economy where the aim of production is not to accumulate profit but to satisfy local needs."[42] Ariyaratne explained a further connection to Buddhist ideology: The ninth item, education, "not only embraces a total life process, but a whole cycle of lives—births and deaths—finally aiming at a state of deathlessness or non-birth."[43] Ariyaratne summarized the list's significance by noting that "the satisfaction of these ten basic needs is the strategy of Sarvodaya [grass-roots]. The final satisfaction of these basic needs in all, leads to the awakening of all."[44]

Shramadana and Awakening

During its first decade, the Sarvodaya Movement employed the Shramadana camp as a vehicle for trying to actualize the Buddhist values of a new social order. Through organizing hundreds of shramadana camps across the country, Sarvodaya taught the rural poor how to liberate themselves by working together on projects that would benefit the community. Ariyaratne reported that more than three hundred thousand volunteers participated in shramadana camps between 1958 and 1966.[45] Typically, shramadana camps were held to build roads, dig wells, or complete some other infrastructure project that a village needed. Sarvodaya taught villagers that the community social action of a shramadana camp facilitates the awakening of the individual and the awakening of the group.

On the individual level, the shramadana experience leads to personality awakening as the volunteers realize the *brahma-vihāras* (Four Divine Abidings). The brahma-vihāras are composed of *mettā* (loving kindness), *karuṇā* (compassion), *muditā* (sympathetic joy), and *upekkhā* (equanimity). Classical Theravada taught that the brahma-vihāras represented enstatic states of mental tranquility that could be reached by withdrawing from the world and practicing *samādhi* (the meditation of calmness). The texts of Theravada describe the process whereby a meditator employing the brahma-vihāras in samadhi could attain the *jhānas* (trance states).

The brahma-vihāras were traditionally cultivated by withdrawing from the world, not by acting in the world. As subjects of meditation they produced calm mental states; creating an ethic for social involvement was not their purpose. The meditator who perfected the mental states of loving kindness or compassion infused these qualities into the world, not by doing social work, but by going through a process that Winston King described as "individualized radiation of virtue and health out into society by holy persons."[46] Sarvodaya, however, teaches that the brahma-vihāras should serve primarily as guidelines for social action. Although the tradition may have seen them as meditation subjects or thoughts, Ariyaratne said this is not sufficient. "Lovingkindness toward all is the thought that an awakening personality should have. But this thought is not enough; it is only the motivation which should lead us to compassionate action."[47]

Clearly, Sarvodaya's engaged Buddhist interpretation has shifted the focus in its understanding of the brahma-vihāras; however, even in classical Theravada these ideas have ethical implications on the mundane, or this-worldly, plane and seem logically to imply a social philosophy.

Ariyaratne maintains that in classical Sri Lankan culture, the awakening of the personality was based on these four principles.[48] Therefore, Sarvodaya promotes them as central elements of its plan for employing the Dharma to assist and uplift the rural poor. Sarvodaya interprets the first principle, mettā, as "respect for all life," cultivating love for all beings. The second principle, karuṇā, which Sarvodaya understands as "compassionate action," follows from mettā. When one acts out of loving kindness and compassion, muditā results as one recognizes the problems of others. Sarvodaya describes joy as an important motive for engaging in the service of society. The fourth principle, upekkhā, becomes important for developing a personality structure that is unshaken by praise or blame, by gain or loss.

On the group level, shramadana facilitates awakening as volunteers work together with compassion and wisdom. Macy noted that, "The genius of shramadana is its capacity to provide a model for the society that Sarvodaya would build. It offers participants the chance to experience—in action and in the present—the kinds of psychological, social, and physical interaction that the Movement considers integral to village awakening."[49] In shramadana camps, village residents join with Sarvodaya volunteers and neighbors to work for a week or more in an atmosphere in which Buddhist values are explicitly cultivated and discussed. Each day of the camp begins and ends with a family gathering, in which ideas such as the brahma-vihāras are considered and the day's work is planned.

During the period of the camp, all participants follow *sangaha vatthūni* (the four grounds of kindness) as the social application of Buddhist ethical ideals. These four principles of group behavior include *dāna* (generosity), *peyyavajja* (kindly speech), *atthacariyā* (useful conduct), and *samānattatā* (equality). Ariyaratne regards these principles as the foundation of traditional village communal life and the antithesis of life in modern, materialist society. Following them leads to a life governed by sharing and nonaggression, as opposed to one governed by individuality and competition. Ariyaratne described the value of these principles for traditional village society when he said, "This social philosophy and practice at the rural level laid a strong infrastructure for the stability and strength of the nation."[50] In a shramadana camp, the participants relate to each other on the basis of these principles and thereby establish a psychological and social infrastructure for authentic development and awakening.

Through living out the brahma-vihāras in the concrete action of shramadana, Sarvodayans implement the path of this-worldly asceticism that leads to the goal of dual liberation. The Buddhist path, including the factors of the Noble Eightfold Path and the brahma-vihāras, constitutes the crucial link between the individual and society in Sarvodaya's scheme of awakening and development, for it provides a means to awaken the self and society together. Ariyaratne said, "To change society we must purify ourselves, and the purification process we need is brought about by working in society."[51]

At times Ariyaratne compares Sarvodaya's conception of the path to that of a bodhisattva, a being who postpones his or her own enlightenment in order to remain in the world to work for the enlightenment of all.[52] The *Bhagavad Gita*'s ideal of a karma yogi, one who sees doing service and work as the highest form of religion, might also be seen, especially as taught by Gandhi, as a central paradigm for Sarvodaya's path.

The exact nature of the interrelationship of individual and social goals in Sarvodaya's vision is illustrated by a saying used by the Movement to describe shramadana camps: "We build the road and the road builds us." This saying expresses Sarvodaya's belief that material development work done on behalf of society also serves spiritual purposes. As Ariyaratne has explained, Sarvodaya actually cannot fail; the road may fail by being washed out, but the awakening that occurred in the building of it will endure. Kantowsky observed that, "Sarvodaya's main message is that human suffering cannot be alleviated merely by material means. Though the Movement tries to organize people to work for material improvements, it has never seen material growth as an answer to man's search for meaning and relevance. All its projects are meant to serve the specific needs of a local community that has been reawakened through Sarvodaya's shramadana techniques to the ancient virtues of interdependent sharing and caring, joint suffering, and compassionate interaction."[53]

Sarvodaya's Growth from a Movement to an Organization: 1967–82

During the second period of its history, Sarvodaya evolved from a work camp movement to a large NGO engaged in village development. The rapid growth occurred for two reasons: the shramadana ideal was popular and Sarvodaya began to receive significant outside funding. The funding fueled Sarvodaya's evolution from a volunteer movement to an organization. The evolution created a shift in the vision and focus: Sarvodaya began to emphasize development more than social revolution as its work increasingly involved village programs and extension projects. To be sure, Sarvodaya did not lose the vision, but as an organization it became more pragmatic about the means and ends of social change. Sarvodaya forged ties and, by the end of the period, became closely allied with the government in its village development work. During this second period, Sarvodaya focused on expansion and development, beginning with the village and later enlarging its scope to include the nation and world.

Village Development

The event that began Sarvodaya's expansion was its Hundred Villages Development Scheme, launched in 1967 to mark the 1969 birth centenary of Mahatma Gandhi. Under this plan, Sarvodaya selected one hundred villages across the country and organized shramadanas and *gramodaya* (village awakening or village development) in each. This campaign served as a laboratory for refining the village-development techniques that Sarvodaya would employ in thousands of villages in the next few years.

During the initial step of the Scheme, Sarvodaya carefully selected a village and conducted a preliminary survey of its needs. Then Sarvodaya organized a shramadana camp to unite the villagers in working on a project that would benefit the village. The shramadanas then, like the shramadanas since, served to lay the foundation for the physical, spiritual, and social infrastructures that were necessary for village awakening.

Shramadanas address physical infrastructural needs through work that is done on common projects. Spiritual or psychological infrastructural needs are addressed through sharing labor and by the daily family gatherings. Describing the significance of these family gatherings, Macy said, "I came to believe that shramadana's distinctive contribution to grassroots development lies in the way it combines physical work with town meetings."[54] In shramadanas and their associated family gatherings, the community has an opportunity to come together, identify new leaders, and give a voice to people, such as women and youth, who had not previously participated in community decisions. These meetings help villagers overcome their sense of helplessness by realizing their vast potential for "self-development based on self-reliance, mutual cooperation, and [the] harnessing of local resources."[55]

Following a shramadana, Sarvodaya prepares the social infrastructure for village development by organizing various groups. They typically include a group for each of the following: preschool children, school-age children, youth, mothers, and farmers. These groups provide peer communities that facilitate the awakening of the members, and they serve to establish some of Sarvodaya's basic services for the village. Sarvodaya stated that "the youth group and the children's group become the driving forces which induce the formation of the other groups also."[56] The extent to which the youth element, which represents the origins of the movement, remained important as Sarvodaya expanded is clear. The youth group motivates youth to work for the improvement of the village and gives them leadership training.

In most villages, one of the first services Sarvodaya develops is a preschool, which draws upon the preschool and mother's groups for students, teachers, funding and support in general. Sarvodaya recognized that a large percentage of children in rural areas did not have access to preschools, so it started organizing them to provide basic education for children between the ages of three and six years. Sarvodaya hired and trained young women from the village as preschool teachers, thereby extending the benefit of the preschools for the village.

Alongside the preschools, Sarvodaya organizes community kitchens to provide basic nutrition for the children. The kitchens offer food and milk, including *kola kenda* (leaf porridge), which Sarvodaya popularized. The preschools also provide a base for a community health emphasis in the village. Mothers received health and nutrition information, and everyone in the village has access to basic health care, first aid, and preventive medicine. Other services facilitated by the preschool and the mother's group include home garden support through information and seed distribution, food banks for the needy, and training in home economics for parents and youth.[57]

Clearly, the preschool program has been one of Sarvodaya's most successful endeavors. Since it is typically one of the first activities that Sarvodaya organizes in a village, the preschool has become the most widespread symbol of the Movement. In 1975 Sarvodaya was operating 472 preschools. By 1999 it had over five thousand preschools. In Sri Lanka, which has a high rate of literacy and values education, Sarvodaya's preschools have been well received and regarded as important contributions to the society.

The groups that Sarvodaya organizes constitute the village Sarvodaya Shramadana Society and provide the basis for village revitalization and awakening. Macy noted that the youth and mother's groups provide opportunities for women to expand their participation in village society: "Sarvodaya's meetings, from Mother's Groups to community 'family gatherings,' give women the opportunity to speak up and share their experiences and ideas. They are expected to express themselves, even though this has not been the cultural norm."[58] Sarvodaya's groups and programs have empowered women to take leadership roles in the Movement; today many of Sarvodaya's village societies are led by women. Early in its evolution, Sarvodaya set up a national center for the Women's Movement in order to assist women in these village groups.

The establishment of all of these groups generates many positive benefits for the village. The children's groups promote savings accounts for children, and the youth groups organize activities and provide various kinds of training for young people. Macy reported that these groups also help the villages address problems such as drinking and gambling: "Sarvodaya's effect on patterns of drinking and gambling is a factor in the allegiance the Movement wins among rural women."[59]

Ariyaratne described the nature of Sarvodaya's development strategy by saying, "In effect, Sarvodaya Shramadana releases a series of developmental processes, the cumulative result of which is a mass movement of mutual help among village communities to improve their quality of life."[60] As Macy said, Sarvodaya's village development activities enable villagers to "move out of patterns of apathy and dependence."[61] One of the most important kinds of awakening that Sarvodaya seeks to facilitate is an awakening to self-reliance and janashakti.

To support the villages that began programs under the Hundred Villages Development Scheme, Sarvodaya established Gramodaya Centers, regional development centers. By 1977 the Movement had established fifty Gramodaya Centers in the various districts of Sri Lanka, and later added more. Each center had one or more Sarvodaya staff members who served as advisors to the villages of the area on matters such as shramadanas, development projects, and the organization of preschools. At the Gramodaya Centers and the headquarters in Moratuwa, Sarvodaya offered various kinds of training for people from the village Sarvodaya groups. These courses provided instruction for preschool teachers and community kitchen workers, and training in community development techniques, rural public health, and various trades.

The Hundred Villages Development Scheme was so successful that by 1971 the Movement was conducting shramadanas and village awakening programs in four hundred villages, and had already set a new target of working in one thousand villages within the next five years.[62] In 1969, as a result of the success of the Movement, Ariyaratne received the Ramon Magsaysay International Award for Community Leadership. This recognition from the Philippines brought increased prestige to the Movement and its leaders.

Financial Support

At the beginning of Sarvodaya's second period of history, the Movement still lived very simply. Even though its work was expanding into many new villages, there was little outside funding; only the voluntary contributions from urban Sri Lankans, some assistance from the government, and a great pool of young volunteers eager to assist with village development provided support. However, with the success of the village development campaign and international recognition, Sarvodaya began to receive financial support from new sources.

In 1972 Sarvodaya was legally incorporated as an NGO. In that year it received its first outside funding from two European foundations, who granted Rs250 thousand for its development work.[63] Also in that year, Ariyaratne resigned from his faculty post at Nalanda College and devoted his time to leading the young Sarvodaya Movement. Although Sarvodaya was able to hire some paid staff at this time, the heart of the Movement remained in the hundreds of young volunteers who were attracted by its Buddhist and Gandhian ideals of service. Volunteers worked without salary and lived among the villagers they were assisting. Reflecting on this period, Ariyaratne said,

> "The transformation of the activities of a set of volunteers into a legally recognized organization gave a considerable impetus to the Movement and contributed very significantly to its quantitative expansion. In hindsight it may now be seen that the creation of the legal entity also created a dichotomy resulting in the Movement on one side and the organization on the other with the latter's growth not always accompanied by a growth of the former."[64]

From that point on, Sarvodaya's outside funding grew exponentially and certainly fueled the growth of the organization, if not the Movement itself. By the mid-1970s Sarvodaya was receiving funding from a half dozen foundations. The largest amounts came from the Netherlands Organization for International Development (NOVIB), the German foundation Friedrich Naumann Stiftung (FNS), and Helvetas in Switzerland. The relations between Sarvodaya and the donors were excellent during this period. The donors may not have completely understood or agreed with Sarvodaya's development aims, but they regarded the Movement as a bold and promising experiment in development: the ideal kind of Asian development movement for northern donor organizations to be supporting. The relationship was beneficial both to the donors and to Sarvodaya.[65] In fact, several of the donor foundations, especially NOVIB, showcased the example of Sarvodaya in their own campaigns to raise foundation funds. By 1980 Sarvodaya was receiving over Rs30 million in support from over a dozen foreign foundations.

The Development of Infrastructure

The growth of outside funding enabled Sarvodaya to expand at both its periphery and its center. While the village development work was growing, Sarvodaya also found it necessary to build a huge infrastructure of administrative centers and training centers to support the village work. For example, it built a world-class Development Educational Institute and Farm in Tanamalwila that had facilities for 400 trainees. This institute, which specialized in appropriate technology and leadership training, embodied the enthusiasm and potential of the Movement to bring change to the villages. Other Development Education Institutes were established in Kandy and Baddegama.

As another aspect of this expansion, Sarvodaya received funds from FNS to build a leadership training institute for Buddhist monks that opened in 1974. Located in the hill country about one hour from Colombo, the Bhikkhu Training Institute was designed to train a cadre of *bhikkhus* (monks) who would be village leaders and could assist in village development. Sarvodaya discovered that monks often played key roles in organizing development, but they needed more training to become effective advocates of development.

Under the leadership of an influential monk, the Venerable H. Ñānasīha, the new Bhikkhu Training Center held great promise for the Movement and the country. Its fine facilities included classrooms, a library, and dining and residential halls for sixty bhikkhus. Although the center prospered for a few years, it began to have problems recruiting and retaining well-qualified bhikkhus. The best-qualified bhikkhus preferred to go to the university rather than the training center; those who did come to the center were from a less-educated group. The first principal of the institute compared these bhikkhus to a set of "untrained buffaloes." Nandasena Ratnapala described the situation at this center in 1976 by saying, "There is no doubt that the training has been a limited success."[66]

Other ventures were more successful, however, as Sarvodaya expanded the kinds of services it offered from the central organization. In 1975 it founded the Sarvodaya Suwasetha Sewa Society to aid orphan and destitute children as well as handicapped and aged adults. Other programs, such as the Sarvodaya Women's Movement and the Shanthi Sena Services, or Peace Brigades, were set up to help the village societies.

The most striking example of donor funded growth was Sarvodaya's 1978 construction of a new headquarters complex and campus in Moratuwa. Demonstrating both its success and its mission, Sarvodaya commissioned a large, striking complex built in the shape of an octagon representing the eight-sided wheel of Dharma, a symbol of the Noble Eightfold Path. The buildings house training centers, a library, media center, conference hall, residence halls, and administrative offices. A sign on the front of this new headquarters complex declares:

> This abode of young men and women trainees who strive to establish a Sarvodaya social order in Sri Lanka and the world in keeping with the noble eightfold path of the Buddhist philosophy is named the *Damsak Mandira* and it is built in the shape of the *Dhamma Chakka* [Wheel of Doctrine].

The construction of the headquarters complex symbolized Sarvodaya's new understanding of its role. The Movement now emphasized not only individual awakening and village awakening, but also the awakening of the nation and the world. With the rapid growth of the Movement into thousands of rural villages, Sarvodaya's leaders had come to appreciate the potential power of the Movement on the national level. Sarvodaya's new national presence was authenticated when President J. R. Jayawardene attended the opening of the Damsak Mandira in 1978. In that same year, Sarvodaya displayed its international aspirations by sponsoring an International Conference on Sarvodaya and Development. The conference drew participants from around the world, who heard the Prime Minister of Sri Lanka, R. Premadasa, praise the Movement's work. In 1982 the international credentials of the Movement were boosted again when Ariyaratne received the King Baudouin Award from Belgium for international development.

Clearly, Sarvodaya had evolved as an organization and now seemed to have great potential for the future. At the beginning of this period it had been working in less than one hundred villages. By the end of the period it reported it was working in over four thousand villages. Sarvodaya now had a hierarchy of administrators in a network of centers: It had developed nine regional centers presiding over twenty-seven district centers, which in turn presided over three-hundred Gramodaya Centers directly overseeing the work in thousands of villages.

The combination of rapid growth through outside funding and the affiliation with the government's development programs, however, eventually led Sarvodaya to a crisis of identity. Sarvodaya had to reconsider its mission and its goals. Ariyaratne admits "we realized at the beginning of the second decade itself, the conceptual contradiction we were developing by the extension approach we were voluntarily following."[67] The process of reconsidering Sarvodaya's identity did not take place, however, until the beginning of the next period of its history.

CHAPTER TWO

SARVODAYA'S VISION OF PEACE
IN A CONTEXT OF VIOLENCE

From the outset the Sarvodaya Movement has worked for peace, but in response to the ethnic conflict that has raged in Sri Lanka for more than twenty years, Sarvodaya has made peace a central part of its identity and agenda. Sarvodaya's peace movement represents a Gandhian-Buddhist response to the conflict, and through this response Sarvodaya has pursued the two pivotal goals of the Movement: liberation and power. These goals fit together in Sarvodaya's program in which spiritual liberation is the base for people's power. Through spiritual liberation people are able to awaken to their true potential and work for peace by countering the structures that have created the conflict.

Sarvodaya's understanding of this twofold quest for peace distinguishes the approach from secular and political efforts. Sarvodaya's peace movement focuses on the need to restore the human spirit and work for peace from the bottom up, rather than attempting to impose it from above. Ariyaratne follows Gandhi in seeking to build this spiritual infrastructure as the key to changing the social and political infrastructure. Sarvodaya's vision of peace draws on Gandhi's commitment to ahimsa and swaraj. Gandhi clearly understood that these values could not exist without changing the violent and oppressive structures of society. The kind of peace Sarvodaya desires is characterized by not merely a return to the status quo, but rather a total social revolution that can reform the values and structures that created the conflict. By building a spiritual infrastructure, Sarvodaya has attempted to "promote an alternative and parallel series of processes within the law leading to a social order which manifests Buddhist values and objectives."[1]

In the 1980s, with the ethnic conflict erupting in the north and economic problems emerging in the south, Ariyaratne and the Sarvodaya Movement protested against the government in much the same way and over many of the same issues as the government's most vocal critics, including some right wing elements of the Buddhist Sangha and

27

the Janatha Vimukti Peramuna (JVP).[2] However, while the JVP and others called for a violent response to the "terrorism," Sarvodaya called for peace and a nonviolent revolution.

Sarvodaya's vision of peace also finds a rich resource in the classical Theravada Buddhist teachings, which Ariyaratne regards as cognates of the Gandhian ideals. The Buddha has been called the *Santi Rājā,* (King of Peace). He taught that peace begins with the individual and then radiates outward into the world as *samācariya* (peaceful living with all beings). In Buddhism, the central datum for peace is the mind; the definitive statement about the centrality of the mind is found in the first two verses of the *Dhammapada*. These verses have been viewed as answers to the questions, What is the source of violence or peace? and What is the source of suffering or happiness?

> "Mind is the forerunner of all realities. Mind is the chief and all are mind made. If anyone speaks or acts with an impure mind, suffering follows him as the wheel follows the foot of the ox. Mind is the forerunner of all realities . . . If anyone speaks or acts with a pure mind, contentment/peace follows him like his never-departing shadow."[3]

According to Theravada Buddhism, there can be no true happiness for the individual without this kind of inner peace, and there can be no true harmony for society without individuals who teach and exemplify the qualities of peace. The Buddha taught that, "when the five hindrances have been put away . . . then [a person] is filled with a sense of peace and in that peace his heart is content."[4] By controlling the mind and attaining inner peace, an individual is able to control her reactions to others, and thereby live by nonviolence. For example, the Buddha taught his followers, "If anyone should give [you] a blow with his hand, . . . with a stick, [or] . . . with a weapon, . . . even so you should get rid of those desires that are worldly, those thoughts that are worldly, and you . . . should train yourself thus: 'Neither will my mind become perverted, nor will I utter an evil speech, but kindly and compassionate will I dwell with a mind of friendliness [mettā] and void of hatred."[5] Buddhism clearly teaches that this kind of nonviolence represents the only path to peace. As the *Dhammapada* says, "Hatred never ceases by hatred; hatred ceases by love (non-hatred). This is the eternal dhamma."[6]

Another key to peace in Buddhist teachings is the realization of *anattā* (selflessness) and its attendant virtue, nonattachment. Buddhism suggests that conflict is most often caused by the ego and desires. By giving up the ego and its attachments one finds peace. The *Dhammapada* says,

"He abused me, he struck me, he overpowered me, he robbed me. Those who harbor such thoughts do not gain peace from their hatred. But . . . those who do not harbor such thoughts still their hatred."[7] Another verse from the *Dhammapada* expresses this classical Buddhist ideal of a nonattached, nonviolent peace: "Victory creates enmity [in the defeated], the defeated live in distress; The peaceful rest happily, having given up both victory and defeat."[8]

All of these Buddhist values related to peace have found expression in the philosophy of the Sarvodaya Movement where they blend with the Gandhian ideals. Sarvodaya maintains that the process of personality awakening or spiritual awakening begins with the individual and then moves to the family, the community, and beyond because all of these levels are interconnected. In this awakening process the individual strives to realize the truths of *paticca samuppāda* (interdependence) and *anattā*, insights that lead to living without attachment and enable one to affirm nonviolence and work for peace. Ariyaratne explained that being nonviolent does not mean being inactive. He said, "We have demonstrated an active nonviolence," and also explained that "to be active in a [violent] situation like that and to work in a nonviolent and nonsectarian way you need great spiritual power."[9]

For Ariyaratne, this kind of spiritual power represents the common denominator of Gandhian and Buddhist thought, as well as the core of all religions. This ecumenical spirituality relates directly to the campaign for peace because, Ariyaratne maintains, the achievement of peace depends on the ability to actualize spiritual unity. Ariyaratne described all religions as "intrinsically messages of peace and brotherhood."[10] The goal of Sarvodaya's peace marches and the meditations that Ariyaratne has led during them has always been "to create a critical mass of spiritual consciousness and then create conditions to sustain that level."[11] In Ariyaratne's view, transforming the consciousness of individuals and communities toward compassion and peace represents an essential step toward building a just and peaceful world.[12]

By creating this critical mass of spiritual consciousness, Sarvodaya attempts to "transfer power to the people" and challenges the structures and parties that have created the violence. Ariyaratne has contended that the conditions permitting violence arose as a result of the colonial period in Sri Lanka. Sri Lanka's postcolonial governments, for the most part, have continued the same approach as their colonial mentors, pursuing centralized social, political, and economic programs that run counter to the Buddhist spirituality that had traditionally guaranteed peace. Ariyaratne wrote "When Sri Lanka was Buddhist, both in precept and practice, there was no need to talk of peace making because there was no fundamental value crisis in Sri Lankan society, in spite of internally or externally caused strife and power struggles . . . Peace prevailed in the minds of the general public and their communities because the generally accepted value system remained unattacked by contending groups." He went on to say that "legalized structural violence prevails and extra legal violent methods are used as well to resolve conflicts."[13] Ariyaratne's appeal to the past has served to critique the contemporary government and empower liberation and reform. The peace movement represents an integral part of Sarvodaya's Gandhian-Buddhist revolution. Sarvodaya's peace movement attempts to awaken the people's spiritual consciousness and restore Buddhist/spiritual values in order to counter the dominant material values that have led to violent structures and the oppression of the people. Macy notes that "the belief that a root problem of poverty is a sense of powerlessness"[14] is implicit in Sarvodaya's goal of awakening. The same assumption underlies the peace movement, for it has represented an extension of Sarvodaya's basic quest to "Awaken people to their *swashakti* (personal power) and *janashakti* (collective or people's power)."[15]

A History of Sarvodaya's Peace Movement: 1983–97

Sarvodaya's emphasis on a peace movement began in July 1983 when the ethnic conflict that had been simmering in Sri Lanka for many years erupted into fiery riots. Reacting to atrocities by Tamil militants in the north, Sinhala militants in the south rioted, burning the homes and businesses of Tamils in a number of towns and cities in the southern and central parts of the island. Many were killed and thousands were left homeless by the rioting, which went on for several days leaving the country paralyzed and in shock. The escalation of the violence in the country thrust Sarvodaya into a major role as a peace broker; the Movement's response to these terrible riots came straight from its Gandhian-Buddhist heritage of nonviolence and peace. Within twenty-four hours after the first riots in Colombo, Sarvodaya began to organize camps for the refugees and aid for the victims.

Since Sarvodaya had been active in all parts of the island, including the Tamil areas, from an early period of its history, it could claim with accuracy to have been attempting to overcome ethnic differences even before the conflict exploded into riots. Tamils have held prominent positions of leadership in Sarvodaya, and Sarvodaya has organized shramadana camps and training programs of various kinds for Tamil youths. Tamils who have worked with Sarvodaya have not regarded it as a Sinhala Buddhist organization, but as a Sri Lankan organization, although some Tamils outside of the Movement have perceived Sarvodaya as Buddhist.

By all accounts, Sarvodaya was very successful in its development programs in the northern part of the island before July 1983.[16] For this reason, Sarvodaya's major donor agencies encouraged Sarvodaya to begin a larger and more comprehensive program of relief in the northern and eastern sectors. These donors viewed Sarvodaya as one of the only organizations that had both the network and the ability to carry out this relief work. The donors' encouragement was one of the major factors that motivated Sarvodaya to assume a national role at that time.

As an immediate response to the riots in 1983, Sarvodaya began working with the government and with other NGOs to plan a peace conference. On October 1, 1983, Sarvodaya convened a major conference to discuss the causes of the conflict and find the path to peace. Some two thousand people representing all segments of Sri Lankan society came together in the Bandaranaike Memorial International Conference Hall, the largest venue in the country. Delegates came from all of the major political parties, religious groups, Sinhala, Tamil, and Muslim communities, and all strata of society. At the end of the two-day conference delegates unanimously adopted a People's Declaration for National Peace and Harmony.[17]

The Declaration clearly reflects the Sarvodaya viewpoint in the way it frames the problems and the solutions. That Sarvodaya was able to stage a national conference and have over two thousand delegates endorse its agenda for resolving the conflict is a testament to the national prominence that Sarvodaya had attained by the early 1980s. At that time, when people in Sri Lanka discussed possible successors to President Jayawardene, "the name of Ahangamage Tudor Ariyaratne and the Sarvodaya Movement of which he is the leader, often crop[ped] up."[18]

Ariyaratne explained that the entire Declaration was written "following Buddhist principles,"[19] although the delegates were said to represent all religious communities. Again, this points to Ariyaratne's belief that there is an underlying spiritual unity to all religions. Sarvodaya's Buddhist values are evident in the introduction to the Declaration, which expresses the importance of reestablishing the Law of Dharma and people's power, so that the country can again be called "the Land of Plenty and an Island of Righteousness *(Dhammadīpa)*." These are Buddhist ideals, to be sure, which were drawn from the heritage of Sinhala Buddhism and may have been understood thus by many of the delegates. However, according to Ariyaratne's interpretation they represent ecumenical spiritual values and national ideals, rather than exclusively Buddhist values.

The Declaration and the Four Noble Truths

The Declaration follows "the Buddha's approach to problems, namely the Four Noble Truths."[20] In the Declaration, the First Noble Truth is equated with the degeneration of Sri Lankan society due to the decline of the traditional value system and the ensuing disruption of the social fabric. This theme is a central element of Sarvodaya's analysis of the problem. Ariyaratne noted that the value system was based on the ancient Hindu-Buddhist codes that "accepted the postulates of respect for life and in particular respect for human life." It generated a spiritual culture that followed the Five Precepts and reached its peak "during the eras in which the influence of Buddhism was felt at its highest."[21] The Declaration states that the emergence of violent groups who have no respect for the Buddhist precepts, or even for human life itself, provides evidence of the decline of traditional values. It also notes that "foreign powers [began] to show undue concern in our internal problems causing a threat to National Sovereignty."[22] This comment reflects the growing concern at the time about the possibility that India might intervene with a peacekeeping force. The possibility was realized in 1987.

The Declaration defines the cause of the suffering, the Second Noble Truth, as colonial imperialism and the decline of the nation following Sri Lanka's independence. Commenting on the argument in the Declaration, Ariyaratne charges that Western imperialism undermined the traditional "spiritual culture" as it replaced the traditional agricultural economy with a commercial culture.[23] He critiques the emphasis that was given to the English language and how it came to replace Sinhala and Tamil as the official language. English was important for commercial culture and the interests of the British, but in Ariyaratne's view the ensuing neglect of the indigenous languages weakened the "well-springs" from which the people had traditionally drawn their "spiritual nourishment."[24]

A related cause, according to the Declaration, was the destruction of the traditional educational system in which "the religious institutions" functioned as the centers of education and "the monks supplied their leadership."[25] Other examples of societal degeneration included the erosion of traditional social norms and the rise of political parties. The partisan political leaders divided the people and weakened the community leadership, including especially "the value-based leadership of the Maha Sangha."[26] In keeping with Sarvodaya's emphasis on the interconnectedness of spirituality and liberation, Buddhist and Gandhian themes dominate the Declaration's diagnosis of the conflict.

It is interesting that both the Declaration and Ariyaratne himself identified the English language as one of the central factors responsible for destroying the culture and creating the conflict. Other observers have traced the linguistic roots of the conflict to the postcolonial Sri Lankan government's "Sinhala-only" language policies. The policies divided the population by giving priority to the Sinhala language and establishing separate schools for Sinhala and Tamil speakers. Taking Ariyaratne's viewpoint, however, the Declaration regards colonialism in general, and its emphasis on English in particular, as the prior cause of the demise of traditional values and community harmony. The Declaration reasons that the emphasis on English education favored a privileged, Western-oriented elite and caused a sharp decline in "the number of community leaders capable of providing leadership from village level up to national level based on People's Power and the Power of Righteousness *[dharma]*."[27]

Although one could debate the explanations given by Ariyaratne and the Declaration of the causes of the nation's problems, there is no doubt that the basic picture they drew was essentially true. Colonialism certainly did decimate the system of subsistence agriculture and family farms that had dominated the traditional economy. Imperialist factors also created an elite class that adopted the English language and Western values. The new economy and the emerging elite generated a competitive system that led to social unrest. Ariyaratne argues that what he views as the traditional spiritual culture was destroyed by these Western influences and that "spiritual life gradually drew away from the rest of social life, and a society almost wholly tending towards commercial values took its place."[28] Cut off from their spiritual values and unable to realize the material desires that the new economy aroused, the people at the bottom of the system naturally felt frustrated and angry.

The Declaration's discussion of the solution and the path to the solution, its analogues to the Third and Fourth Noble Truths, clearly reflects the Sarvodaya Movement's agenda for peace and social reform. The Declaration calls for reestablishing the spiritual, moral, and cultural values, "as traditionally laid down under the leadership of the Maha Sangha," and reforming the (traditionally Buddhist) educational system. Once the values have been established, economic and political reforms that reflect Sarvodaya's vision of social revolution will follow. The Declaration endorses Sarvodaya's call for the economic system to be revised to "reestablish a suitable economic lifestyle, simple, plain, and sustainable." With regard to the political system, the Declaration recommends creating "without further delay an alternative political system in-keeping with our values and needs, in place of the party based system which is a Western product and is one of the primary causes of the degeneration of the . . . present society."[29] These proposals foreshadowed the more comprehensive call for social and political reform that Ariyaratne would make a few years later in his book, *The Power Pyramid and the Dharmic Cycle*. Overall, in the explication of all of the Four Noble Truths, the Declaration supports Sarvodaya's view that the road to peace lies through social revolution.

Working for Peace

Following the conference, Ariyaratne endeavored to implement its aim "to create a spiritual, mental, social, and intellectual environment" for peace in the nation by undertaking a Gandhian peace march or "peace walk" from the southern tip of the island to Jaffna and Nagadeepa in the north. The final section of the Declaration called for such a march, saying it would release a great "Spiritual Force . . . from the minds of the thousands that would participate in this Peace Walk."[30] The walk was scheduled to begin on December 6, 1983, and as the date approached, thousands of representatives from all of Sri Lanka's ethnic groups began assembling at Kataragama in southern Sri Lanka. The march would cover a thousand miles in one hundred days and pass through some of the most troubled areas of the country. Its plans put Sarvodaya in the national and international spotlight.

Ultimately, however, the march did not come to pass. Led by Ariyaratne, ten thousand marchers had gone only a few miles when President J. R. Jayawardene contacted them and requested them to stop. Jayawardene's stated reason for stopping the march was that he feared it would disrupt the work of the government's peace negotiations at the impending All Party Conference. Jayawardene also said privately that the government had information that terrorists were plotting to assassinate Ariyaratne during the march in order to cause further rioting by the Sinhalese. Sarvodaya, therefore, halted the march to prevent further violence.[31]

After the first peace march was cancelled, however, Ariyaratne and Sarvodaya continued to pursue the path of peace in the following months and years. They organized other major and minor peace marches, including two massive marches to Sri Pada in 1985 and 1986. During both of these marches, over thirty thousand people representing all of the religious and ethnic communities of Sri Lanka walked through the hill country and up the sacred mountain. A few years later, in 1990, Sarvodaya organized an even larger march from Kandy to Sri Pada. These peace marches had great symbolic value at a time when most people in the country longed for peace, but felt helpless in the face of increasing violence.

The peace marches symbolized Ariyaratne and his supporters' protest against the terrorists. During one march Ariyaratne said, "Let it be known to those who bear arms that there are about two million members in Sarvodaya who are prepared to brave death anywhere and anytime."[32] From the Sarvodaya perspective, the marches healed the spirit and restored unity

among the people. They always included a guided loving kindness meditation dedicated to all beings. In these group meditations, Ariyaratne taught
marchers to reflect on this truth: "The noblest characteristic of a human
being is so to control thought, word, and action with intelligence and
mental alertness so that they do not cause oneself or others any violence,
repression, or harm [because] like oneself, all other beings too dislike
violence . . . [and] like to live in a peaceful environment."[33]

In 1987, when the presence of a large Indian Army peacekeeping force
complicated the situation in Sri Lanka, Sarvodaya launched a program that
it called the People's Peace Offensive (PPO). The PPO was conceived as
an alternative to the political and military attempts at creating a solution
to the conflict. Ariyaratne described this as "an active intervention by
organized groups of peace loving people . . . confronting violence with nonviolence."[34] This offensive proposed dialogue between all sides to set the
stage for an effective cease-fire. The cease-fire would be monitored by PPO
committees. The program's plan also included various kinds of relief and
rehabilitation, such as reopening schools, hospitals, and religious institutions. The overall aim was to alleviate suffering and "soften the hearts
of both sides to stop the violence," so that a lasting peace could be established. Although the PPO has taken a lower profile since the Indian forces
withdrew in the late 1980s and Sarvodaya came under attack by
Premadasa's government (see Chapter Four), it established a pattern of
ongoing peace activities by the Sarvodaya Movement.

The continuing peace initiatives that Sarvodaya carried out included
relief work in the war zones. Sarvodaya established a program called the
"Five Rs": Relief, Rehabilitation, Reconciliation, Reconstruction, and
Reawakening. Through this program the Sarvodaya Movement shifted its
work in the conflict areas from a focus on development to one of relief for
people displaced by the war. These activities were carried out by Sarvodaya
workers in eleven districts in the north and east, including Ampara,
Batticaloa, Jaffna, Kalmunai, Kantale, Kilinochchi, Mannar, Mullaitivu,
Trincomalee, Vavuniya South and Vavuniya North.[35] Sarvodaya used its
village network to provide food for the refugees, conduct medical clinics,
construct shelters, and rebuild houses and schools for those affected by the
conflict. Other activities included tree planting campaigns, sewing classes,
and trauma counseling.

In 1988, a grant from three foreign donor agencies (Netherlands Organization for International Development Cooperation; the Canadian International Development Agency; and the Intermediate Technology
Development Group) enabled Sarvodaya to expand the scope of its work
in the north and east. It began a new program called Relief, Rehabilitation,
Reconstruction, and Development (RRR&D). Its goal was to set up a

process whereby Sarvodaya would administer relief while gradually trying to return these areas to normal development activities.[36] Although Sarvodaya's district coordinator in Jaffna was killed by terrorists in 1986, the Movement continued to work in the north and east as much as possible throughout the conflict. Its staff came from the Tamil community and demonstrated the ethnic diversity of the Movement.

During the 1992–93 fiscal year, Sarvodaya gave relief supplies to more than seventy-five thousand families and set up thirty-two camps for displaced persons. At the end of 1993, however, the outside funding for the RRR&D program ended and Sarvodaya had to reduce its staff in these areas by one hundred and eighteen workers. After making those cuts, each Sarvodaya district center in the north and east was left with only two staff members. Still, the relief operations continued on a somewhat smaller scale, often in conjunction with the United Nations relief efforts.[37] Ariyaratne noted that the relief work represents an expression of Sarvodaya's "active nonviolence." This work, essential to meet the short term needs of the people, contributed to Sarvodaya's vision of a long term solution at the village level.

Sarvodaya's peace initiatives also included the development of Shanti Sena, a youth brigade for peace. Shanti Sena has assisted in many of Sarvodaya's programs for peace and national harmony. A chief activity has been its youth exchange plan, in which Sinhala youth from the south and Tamil youth from the north spend three months in each other's villages. This kind of community bridge building represents a key component of Sarvodaya's strategy for peace. As part of its decentralization plan, Sarvodaya has made Shanti Sena an independent branch of the Movement.

Diplomacy and Recognition

To move the peace process forward, Ariyaratne made two trips to Jaffna during the conflict, first in 1994 and again in 1997. Since formal negotiations between the government and the Liberation Tigers of Tamil Eelam (LTTE)[38] were not occurring during this time, Ariyaratne's goodwill missions represented important attempts to bring both parties to the negotiating table. During the 1994 trip, Ariyaratne and his colleagues met with some of the LTTE leaders, where Ariyaratne volunteered his services as a mediator between the LTTE and the government. They also visited hospitals. Returning from Jaffna, Ariyaratne reported that he was well received and that the people expressed a desire for a peaceful settlement of the conflict.

In 1997, after the Sri Lankan army had recaptured Jaffna from the LTTE and occupied the city, Ariyaratne made a second trip to the north. This time he went in his new capacity as a member of the government's Human Rights Commission to help establish a human rights center in Jaffna. During the trip he met with community leaders, including the Bishop of Jaffna, other local leaders, and the Army commanders. While in Jaffna, Ariyaratne took steps to reestablish the Sarvodaya center that had been damaged during the fighting. Upon his return, he called for people in the south to come to the aid of people in the north.[39]

During the 1990s, as a result of his leadership of Sarvodaya's peace movement, Ariyaratne received two prestigious international awards. The first was the 1992 Niwano Peace Prize from Japan's Niwano Peace Foundation, which is affiliated with the Rissho Kosei-kai Buddhist sect. The prize is awarded annually to a person or group that has "contributed to peace in the spirit of religion." The Niwano Foundation recognized Ariyaratne for his dedication to peace, demonstrated by his thirty years of service to the villagers and his relief and reconciliation work during the conflict. The second prize, the Gandhi Peace Prize, was awarded in 1996 by the government of India. India established this award in 1995, on the 125th anniversary of Mahatma Gandhi's birth. It is awarded annually for "social, economic, and political transformation through nonviolence and other Gandhian methods."[40] The award committee recognized Ariyaratne for applying Gandhi's principles to contemporary problems and working selflessly for peace and nonviolence. Ariyaratne was the second recipient of the prize.

In his award acceptance speeches, Ariyaratne spoke about the connections between Gandhian and Buddhist approaches to peace and development. Reflecting on Sri Lanka's inheritance of the Buddha's teachings from India, he said, "So it is not strange that once again Sri Lanka should take with gratitude from India the teaching and practices of Mahatma Gandhi and give them new life through Sarvodaya."[41] He noted that the current social structures and the forces of globalization do not build peace and justice; what is needed is "a global transformation of human consciousness as Lord Buddha and Mahatma Gandhi conceived."[42]

These international peace prizes represented official recognition of the national and international role that both Ariyaratne and Sarvodaya had attained. During this period, Ariyaratne had become one of the leading advocates in Sri Lanka, not only of peace, but also of the kinds of social change necessary for peace. With this new national stature, he spoke out against the government and blamed the political parties for the current situation. He also criticized the Buddhist establishment, arguing that Sri Lanka—in its present form—was not a Buddhist country. "Even though historically and culturally Sri Lanka may claim to be Buddhist, in my opinion, certainly the way political and economic structures are instituted and managed today they can hardly be called Buddhist either in precept or practice."[43] Although Sarvodaya had had cordial relations with most of the Sri Lankan governments, Ariyaratne's high profile and his criticisms led to conflicts with the government of President Premadasa (see Chapter Four).

An example of the Premadasa government's opposition to Sarvodaya occurred when the Niwano Peace Foundation decided to award the Niwano Peace Prize to Ariyaratne. As soon as the Japanese government announced the award recipient, the Sri Lankan Ambassador in Japan protested, saying the foundation should not give the prize to Ariyaratne. Instead it should rescind the award because Ariyaratne was under investigation by a governmental commission and, more importantly, he had recently "taken to political activities."[44] After Ariyaratne issued a press release questioning the justice of both the charges and this interference by the government, the Foreign Ministry released a statement that "categorically denied" that the ambassador had tried to lobby for the withdrawal of the award. The foundation, ignoring the controversy, awarded the prize to Ariyaratne as announced.

Afterward, however, the Sri Lankan government wrote to Ariyaratne raising tax questions about the cash stipend connected with the award. The prize included a cash award of 20 million yen. Believing that the government might seize the stipend, Ariyaratne arranged for the foundation to defer the award of that portion of the prize to a later date. The stipend was finally awarded two years later, after the Premadasa government had ended and Sarvodaya once again enjoyed good relations with the new government.

Continuing the Peace Initiative: 1997–2002

After Ariyaratne received the awards, he contributed the prize money to a trust fund for the construction of Vishva Niketan, a new peace center. The founding of Vishva Niketan in 1997 marked the beginning of a new peace campaign. Ariyaratne conceived the idea for a center that would serve as a place of meditation and peace. Vishva Niketan represents a physical expression of Sarvodaya's vision that reestablishing a traditional value system or a spiritual infrastructure is essential for peace. Sarvodaya's literature about the peace center states that, "Vishva Niketan is being established in the firm belief that enduring peace can only be attained when the participants achieve inner peace, a cessation of conflict within themselves."[45]

The center comprises a series of meeting rooms, meditation halls, and residence halls all beautifully designed to create a setting where people can pursue both inner and outer peace. Located on a two acre site near the main Sarvodaya headquarters campus, Vishva Niketan provides a serene venue for individuals and groups to study and discuss issues related to peace. Providing a neutral ground for conflict resolution, its facilities can also be used for training mediators and studying various conflicts. Sarvodaya's vision is that the center will be available not only to address the local conflict, but also to assist in resolving international conflicts. The center promotes the "learning, teaching, and practicing of the universal teachings of the Buddha" in order to "contribute to the spiritual revival of human kind in Sri Lanka and throughout the world."[46]

The People's Peace Initiative

In the mid-1990s, when Vishva Niketan was in the planning stages, the Sarvodaya Movement made a decision to reenergize its quest for peace. In the early 1990s, Sarvodaya had focused more on relief work than peace activism while it waited to see what the government's negotiations would produce. Buoyed by the peace awards Ariyaratne won and confronted with the lingering ethnic conflict, however, the Movement decided to address the problem that was destroying the country.

Sarvodaya acted to broaden its peace effort by developing a new programmatic emphasis that it named the People's Peace Initiative.[47] Drawing from forty years of Gandhian-Buddhist experience, Sarvodaya returned to two basic principles:

1. The prerequisite for peace is the building of a spiritual infrastructure: Inner peace must be realized before outer peace.

2. Peace cannot be imposed from the top down, but must be founded on the people's consent, from the bottom up.

Ariyaratne stated the rationale for this new campaign in his Gandhi Peace Prize acceptance speech: "We recognize that the resolution of our war cannot be left to either the politicians or to the military commanders alone. Making peace calls for a realistic assessment of ground realities. Increasing the awareness of people at the grass roots and generating in them a sympathetic feeling for the sufferings of others is one part of changing those ground realities."[48] The incentive for Sarvodaya's becoming proactive in the peace process was also expressed in the Movement's 1992–93 Annual Report, which said, "Sarvodaya believes that while politicians play 'politics' and armies fight battles, the people may get together with people to make both armies and such politicians unnecessary."[49]

Sarvodaya believed that the time was right for the People's Peace Initiative and that it was uniquely positioned to achieve a lasting people's peace. As one writer argued, "Realistically, Sarvodaya is the only existing organization in Sri Lanka that could mobilize the population across ethnic and religious lines."[50] Sarvodaya concluded that it represented the best hope for working for peace from the grass roots. However, some other factors contributed to the opportunity for starting a Sarvodaya peace campaign at that time. One factor was the new leadership that emerged in the Sarvodaya Movement itself: Dr. Vinya Ariyaratne, one of A. T. Ariyaratne's sons, assumed the post of Executive Director. Assembling a team of energetic new leaders, he has facilitated greater support and coordination for the peace movement.

A second factor was the Sri Lankan parliamentary elections of 2001, in which the United National Party regained a majority in the parliament after making campaign promises to reopen peace talks with the LTTE. In February 2002 the new Prime Minister, Ranil Wickremesinghe, met with Tamil leaders to sign a cease-fire document that had been worked out by a Norwegian negotiating team. Ariyaratne noted that in "the three most recent elections held in the country, the people voted in large numbers for political parties with a peace platform. But the reality is that the people are without the power to convert their desires into reality."[51] However, in autumn 2002 the people's desire for peace received a boost when the government and the LTTE actually initiated peace negotiations. The atmosphere for peace was also strengthened in 2001 by the international focus on ending violence and terrorism. Although Sarvodaya's campaign began before this international focus started in September 2001, Sarvodaya may have been encouraged by the international momentum.

To conduct its peace campaign, Sarvodaya established a new department, the Peace Secretariat, and issued a position paper analyzing the situation and setting out a strategy for peace. The paper argues that the war as it is currently being pursued cannot be won by either side; it can only be continued. The paper also suggests that there are three "armies" in Sri Lanka: the government forces, the LTTE, and a third force consisting of "Sarvodaya's staff and volunteers, numbering close to 100,000."[52] The paper set out a Sarvodaya People's Peace Plan that would provide a new approach to the war: "The war cannot be won; it can only be transcended."[53] The most immediate requirement for this peace process is a cease-fire in which all sides stop fighting immediately. Then peace meditations should be employed to accomplish a number of objectives, including "eliminating violence from our own hearts" and envisioning a "peaceful, harmonious, and sustainable Sri Lanka."[54]

To implement this plan, Sarvodaya mobilized its supporters to hold some major peace meditations. The People's Peace Initiative began with a peace march and meditation in August 1999, for which one hundred seventy thousand people from across the island came together in Vihara Maha Devi Park in central Colombo. At that march, Ariyaratne led the ecumenical group in a meditation on nonviolence and unity. Following that initial event, the Sarvodaya Peace Secretariat organized eight other regional peace meditations. Altogether over two hundred fifteen thousand people participated in this campaign for a people's peace.

In January 2002, Sarvodaya announced plans for an even larger gathering. On March 15, Sarvodaya's Peace Samadhi Day in the sacred city of Anuradhapura attracted six hundred fifty thousand people from fifteen thousand Sinhala, Tamil, and Muslim villages to meditate for peace. Joanna Macy, who participated in this event, described it in this way: "Sitting on the grass as far as I could see, 650,000 people made the biggest silence I have ever heard. As the silence deepened, I thought: This is the sound of bombs and landmines not exploding, of rockets not launched, and machine guns laid aside."[55]

Looking Ahead

With these demonstrations, Sarvodaya gave the quest for peace a central place on its agenda. Sarvodaya has employed the peace meditations to move the hearts and minds of people toward nonviolence and compassion. Recognizing that two decades of conflict have created a culture of war that allows people to accept the violence and view it as normal, Sarvodaya has sought to create a culture of peace that makes the violence unacceptable and unthinkable. Its goal is to change the climate so that, for example, adults are not focused on the war and primary-school children do not draw pictures of war and violence.

The peace meditations represent an important first step in a process of healing, reconciliation, and national unity. As a follow-up to them, Sarvodaya plans to facilitate a Village Link-Up Program, in which a thousand Tamil villages will be paired with a thousand Sinhala villages. They will work together to relieve suffering and create unity. It is expected that people from the Sinhala villages will conduct shramadanas in the Tamil villages to help them recover from the devastation of the war. Young people from both sides will also engage in village exchange visits. As of late 2002, however, this program was still on the drawing board.

Sarvodaya takes a long view of this process, describing it as a five-hundred-year peace plan. Macy said, "Sarvodayans point out that the seeds of Sri Lanka's civil war were planted 500 years ago with European colonization, and estimate that healing will require an equal amount of time."[56] Sarvodaya's peace plan projects these goals for this process:

- First, implement a cease-fire and initiate cross-cultural dialogue at the village level.

- After one year, the violence ends, a peace treaty is signed, and development of the dry zone areas begins again as the country invests the "peace dividend."

- After five years, the dry zone development plan is fully implemented and the causes of poverty are addressed.

- After ten years, resettlement of all refugees is complete.

- After fifty years, the army is abolished, allowing Sri Lanka to have the lowest rates of poverty and suicide in the world.

- After one hundred years, Sri Lanka eliminates poverty, "both economic and spiritual."

- After five hundred years, although global climate changes may cause environmental change, the people of Sri Lanka will be able to survive because of their history of working together.[57]

Sarvodaya's Comprehensive Plan for 2000–05 describes the peace initiative as "one of the major roles of Sarvodaya in the new millennium."[58] The Movement retains this emphasis on peace, even now that the peace talks have begun and the cease-fire is in effect; until a peace treaty is signed one cannot assume that peace has arrived or will remain.

Sarvodaya recognizes, however, that attaining peace involves many transformations; peace does not exist in a vacuum. The primacy of spiritual transformation is visible in the Movement's emphasis on peace meditations at its marches and gatherings and in the resources it has committed for the construction of Vishva Niketan. From Sarvodaya's Gandhian-Buddhist perspective, the transformation of consciousness is crucial, because it facilitates transformations of the social, political, and economic structures that lie at the root of the suffering and violence. The transformation of these structures empowers the people to construct a peaceful and just society.

Ariyaratne wrote that the only means to peace is "the dispelling of the view of 'I and mine' or the shedding of 'self' and the realization of the true doctrines of the interconnection between all animal species and the unity of all humanity."[59] Because Sarvodaya recognizes this Buddhist truth of the interdependence of all, it has tied its quest for peace very closely to its overall quest for a nonviolent, village-based people's revolution as ultimately the only way to establish true peace. It is to an examination of Sarvodaya's vision of this nonviolent revolution that the next chapter turns.

CHAPTER THREE

ECONOMIC EMPOWERMENT
AND THE VILLAGE REVOLUTION

The call for a nonviolent, people's revolution has been a key feature of the Sarvodaya Movement from an early period. However, as the Movement evolved, its discourse shifted more to issues of development than revolution. But in the 1980s, with the situation in the country deteriorating, Ariyaratne returned to the theme of revolution. Sarvodaya's revolutionary discourse drew not only on the Gandhian-Buddhist tradition, but also on Ariyaratne's own socialist inclinations. Early in the Movement he declared that "the goal of Sarvodaya is complete socialism."[1]

Adhering to both the Gandhian and the Buddhist explanations for suffering, Sarvodaya renewed its call for a dramatic, nonviolent revolution. Ariyaratne issued this call prior to the clash with President Premadasa's government in 1990 and prior to the withdrawal of the major donors' funding for the Movement. When those events occurred, however, they did not dampen Sarvodaya's spirit of revolution; instead they intensified Sarvodaya's commitment to the need for sweeping change. The People's Peace Offensive, launched by Sarvodaya in 1987, was designed to inaugurate a revolution that would challenge the prevailing social, economic, and political structures that were contributing to the suffering in the country.

In reiterating the appeal for a no-poverty, no affluence society in the mid-1980s, Ariyaratne emphasized Sarvodaya's vision of an alternative, simple, and sustainable lifestyle based on reducing material desires. He especially criticized the government's open economic policies for fostering consumerism and widening the gap between the rich and the poor.[2] Because of these policies, the gap had grown so that "the poorest 40% who received 13% of the national income in 1973 received only 7% by 1985, whereas [the share received by] the richest 10% increased from 27% to 50%."[3] Ariyaratne wrote, "The economic goals, structures, and processes that are officially promoted are not . . . conducive to building peace in a Buddhist way. Promoting consumerism is one extreme which

Lord Buddha rejected as *kāmasukhallikānuyoga,* [attachment to world-ly enjoyment]."[4] In a report to its members, Sarvodaya identified three main problems that it sought to address: the "continued impoverishment of the bottom 60 percent of the population," the ethnic conflict, and "the unreachable lifestyle being advertised as the one for the general population to aspire to."[5]

Contrasting Sarvodaya's ideal social system with that of the West, Ariyaratne noted one essential difference: The West defines the standard of living in material terms, while Sarvodaya defines it in spiritual terms. On Sarvodaya's model, the key to changing society is identical to the key to achieving peace: It requires building up a critical mass of spiritual consciousness, or "awakening." Ariyaratne hopes the awakening of individuals and villages will radiate outward and spark a "horizontal global awakening," whereby self-governing communities around the world will set in motion a grassroots social revolution.[6]

In 1988, Ariyaratne published *The Power Pyramid and the Dharmic Cycle*, in which he articulated the call for a spiritual revolution that would replace the present socioeconomic and political structures with a Sarvodaya social order.[7] The book's title reflects Gandhi's essay, "The Pyramid and the Oceanic Circle." In the essay, Gandhi argued that society should not be like a pyramid, with the many at the base supporting the few at the top. Instead it should be an "oceanic circle" of individuals and villages.[8]

In his treatise, Ariyaratne applied Gandhi's model to the conditions in Sri Lanka, arguing against the "power pyramid" of the current political and economic system, in which a minority of the people have been able to usurp the power and wealth of the masses. Very outspoken in his criticism of the situation, Ariyaratne commented, "One does not require explanatory treatises to realise that the prevailing social system is a violent, oppressive system."[9] To correct the situation a total nonviolent revolution is needed to overcome the structural violence created by the current system.

The publication of this book marked a significant milestone in Sarvodaya's evolution: Ariyaratne believed the time had come for the Movement to break with the government and work for a revolution that would bring sweeping changes to the political, economic, and social systems of the country. The basic nature of the changes Ariyaratne envisioned in this book involve a shift to a system of people's participatory democracy or village democracy based on a Gandhian-Buddhist

model.[10] Although the break with the government was repaired somewhat a few years later when a new regime was in power, the ideal of a
nonviolent revolution would remain a powerful theme for Sarvodaya.

The Sinhala Village and Gram Swaraj: A Debate

The village stands at the center of the projected Sarvodaya social order,
and thus is in the forefront of the call for a revolution as set out in *The
Power Pyramid and the Dharmic Cycle*. Focused on the village, Ariyaratne's program for social change stresses decentralization and a bottom-up approach. He has argued that "full human development and
happiness cannot be achieved by centralisation [because] centralisation
as a system is inconsistent with a nonviolent structure of society."[11] As
a Movement, Sarvodaya seeks liberation and awakening, which can be
defined by qualitative states such as happiness, peace, and nonviolence;
states best developed and nurtured in a decentralized system focusing on
the family and the village. Ariyaratne's vision of village-based society is
thoroughly grounded in both Gandhian ideals and Sinhala Buddhist ideology.

Gandhi's ideal of gram swaraj figures prominently in Sarvodaya's discourse where Ariyaratne cites Gandhi's statement, "You cannot build
nonviolence on a factory civilization, but it can be built on self-con-
tained villages."[12] For Ariyaratne as for Gandhi, the village represents
the heart of the nation and the source of its spiritual and moral vision.
Gandhi expressed his view of the village in statements such as this: "It
is in the villages of India where India lives, not in the few Westernized
cities which are the citadels of foreign power."[13]

Gandhi's interpretation of the village's significance extended the
debate about its role in the process of modernization that had begun in
the early nineteenth century. In one of the most influential images, a
British official, Sir Charles Metcalfe described Indian villages in an 1832
government report as "little republics" that were "almost independent
of any foreign relations . . . [and] seem[ed] to last where nothing else
lasts."[14] In 1853 Karl Marx expressed the opposite view: "We must not
forget that these idyllic village communities, inoffensive though they
may appear, had always been the solid foundation of Oriental despotism
. . ."[15] Marx regarded Indian villages as places that enshrined social
inequality, which had an oppressive effect on the people and the nation.

Gandhi clearly followed the romantic depiction by Metcalfe and the
idealization of rural life by Ruskin, rather than the negative views of
Marx. On Gandhi's interpretation, the network of semiautonomous villages represented the solution to the nation's political and economic ills.

Gandhi proposed the *panchayat* (village council) as the ideal system of decentralized government, and he set up his Constructive Program of cottage industries and village social services as the ideal economic system for a free India. Kantowsky noted that these elements constituted essential components of Gandhi's vision of a Sarvodaya Society in which all persons have a place.[16]

For Gandhi, a village-based society and polity was essential both for spiritual progress and for peace. He said, "People will never be able to live at peace with each other in towns and palaces. They will then have no recourse but to resort to both violence and untruth."[17] In Gandhi's view the spiritual values of nonviolence and truth outweighed any material or economic advantages that urbanization and industrialization might offer. Gandhi's Sarvodaya revolution represented an authentic Asian approach to modernization that ennobled the individual and left no one behind. However, his image of a Sarvodaya state was never wholly endorsed by Nehru and the Congress party leaders, who endeavored to industrialize India and viewed Gandhi's idea of a network of village republics as "utopian." Kantowsky asserted that "Gandhi's solution to the conflict between man and the institutions that he creates as a social being was the abolition of the state."[18]

Ariyaratne's Vision of Dhammadīpa

In order to translate Gandhi's idea of a village revolution for a Sri Lankan audience, Ariyaratne combined it with images of village society drawn from the Sinhala Buddhist heritage stemming from the Buddhist chronicles such as the *Mahāvaṃsa*. He depicted the ancient Sri Lankan village as a self-sufficient community where Buddhist and spiritual values were respected and followed. In *The Power Pyramid and the Dharmic Cycle,* he argued for the superiority of this ancient village culture, saying, "what we must bear in mind is that a system capable of organizing human society free from the exploitation of man by man had been discovered and implemented by our forefathers . . . [A] fully socialist Buddhist social system . . . inspired by Buddhism did exist as recently as eleven and a half centuries ago."[19] The four principal Buddhist social virtues guided this village culture: sharing, virtuous speech, right livelihood, and equality.[20]

Ariyaratne points to the Anuradhapura period as a "golden era" when this ancient village culture reached its fulfillment and life was guided not by a quest for material goods, but by "religious and cultural activities."[21] This spiritual development of the ancient village culture enabled the country to become what Ariyaratne refers to as a Dhammadīpa. By sounding

the theme of Dhammadīpa, Ariyaratne invokes the *Mahāvaṃsa's* account
of the Buddha's prophecies that in Sri Lanka the Dharma would be pre-
served.[22] Ariyaratne employs this theme, which played a pivotal role in
the Sinhala Buddhist ideology of Dharmapāla and other reformers, to
demonstrate that Gandhi's image of the village republic may be even more
viable in Sri Lanka than in India.[23]

In addition to painting a romantic or affirmative Orientalist picture of
the ancient village, Ariyaratne also contends that this superior culture still
exists in vestigial form in remote Sri Lankan villages today. Sarvodaya's
aim is not to institute a new plan of development, he explains, but "to
revive the indigenous, age-old perception of reality that the people still
possess and assist them to organize themselves on the basis of their own
resources."[24] Among the values that these vestigial "old societies" continue to embrace Ariyaratne lists "nonviolence, sharing, smallness, decentralization, relevant technologies, production by the masses, and unity."[25]
In the village society the "concept of the well-being of all, the awakening
of all, or what we call Sarvodaya is well understood."[26] According to Ariyaratne, the values only faded because, during the colonial period, Western powers imposed foreign values along with a foreign economic system
on the country.

Continuing the Debate

Ariyaratne's positive image of the Sri Lankan village has been challenged
by critics who have said that "Sarvodaya's attempt to recapture a glorious
past is utopian."[27] Gananath Obeyesekere and Richard Gombrich critiqued Ariyaratne's images of the village as the "creation of tradition."
They wrote, "Sarvodaya's vision of village society and the past of Sri
Lankan civilization is a projection of the bourgeoisie, a fantasy that has
no social reality."[28] Commenting on Ariyaratne's depiction of the peace
and harmony in village society, Obeyesekere and Gombrich suggested
that, "One must conclude that Ariyaratne cannot have lived in a traditional village for any length of time."[29] However, this suggestion is incor-
rect, because Ariyaratne grew up in a small village in southern Sri Lanka
near Galle; he is well acquainted with the nature of village life. His romantic image of the village probably comes from a combination of nostalgia
for the rural culture where his family lived and a strong belief in the Gandhian ideals.

Ariyaratne's positive image of the village and these scholars' critiques
of that image continue the earlier colonial and Gandhian views of the
South Asian village. Obeyesekere and Gombrich adhere to a more or less
Marxist view, echoing his descriptions of ancient-village India as a bar-
baric society that "restrained the human mind" and was dominated by

"distinctions of caste and slavery."[30] Obeyesekere and Gombrich noted the "social conflict" and "abuse that characterize Sinhala village life."[31] Critics such as N. Hennayake, who regard Sarvodaya's projected village revolution as utopian, echo Nehru's view that the Sarvodaya scheme does not represent a viable path to modernization or development.[32]

The Two Levels of Sarvodaya's Discourse

Ariyaratne clearly follows Gandhi and the Buddhist reformers in this debate. One should not necessarily jump to the conclusion, however, as some of Ariyaratne's critics have, that Sarvodaya is "uncritically dependent on a myth of a glorious past" and simply rehearsing the ideology of the dominant Sinhala Buddhist nationalists.[33] The Sarvodaya Movement's discourse about a glorious past or a golden era of village culture seems to function on at least two levels. One is the mythical-ideological level, derived from the *Mahāvaṃsa* and inherited from the Sinhala Buddhist reformers. On this level, there is no doubt that Ariyaratne believes, as many Buddhists do, that ancient Sri Lanka had an advanced Buddhist civilization that flowered during the Anuradhapura and Polonnaruwa periods. Proponents of this idea point to the impressive archaeological evidence that supports their belief.

On another, more relevant level, however, Ariyaratne operates with a demythologized version of the ancient culture's glorious past. He employs the discourse about the ancient culture as a way of both validating the Buddhist and spiritual values behind the myth and authenticating Sarvodaya's Buddhist alternative to Western development. He does not use this discourse to legitimate Sinhala identity or privilege, but to provide a warrant for Sarvodaya's challenge to Western and capitalist values.

For example, conceding that his view of the village may appear somewhat romantic and overly positive, Ariyaratne nevertheless defends this image as a means of lifting up a model that can counter the pervasive influence of Western culture. How else, he argues, will it be possible to convince the rural people that they have a noble heritage and noble values that are worth far more than the Western ideas and values that were introduced with colonialism and continue to influence the national culture? Ariyaratne goes on to ask whether the United States of America, Russia, Japan, or Singapore should be the models that the people of Sri Lanka should emulate, or whether Sri Lankans should follow their own heritage, which enabled people to build the great civilizations of the past. Sarvodaya entered into village development "in order to dispel ignorance, inequality, and powerlessness, and to raise the consciousness of the villagers, making them feel that they are human beings with great potential which needs to be put into action."[34]

In this way, the image of the ancient village functions in Sarvodaya's discourse primarily as a means of advocating Buddhist and spiritual values as the basis for development. Ariyaratne asks, "Given this historical background, to what extent can we implement these moral values in practical terms and in the context of the present-day world?"[35] The village socioeconomic model that Sarvodaya proposes lifts up a Gandhian and Buddhist alternative to the materialist or multinational development models that have been employed in Sri Lanka.[36] In Ariyaratne's view, much of the suffering in rural areas has been the result of development policies that the government has drawn up in conjunction with Western multinational corporations and agencies. Ariyaratne criticizes Western culture for undermining human relationships, promoting materialism, increasing competition, and creating complex, top-down systems that increase human suffering or dukkha. The West has built up "large-scale methods and systems, created by man and capable of dominating man, in place of the simple social, economic, and political institutions which man could dominate."[37]

Although these Western models foster greed, hatred, and delusion, Sarvodaya's Buddhist social system seeks to remove these poisons. Countering greed, the village model is radically nonmaterialist, following the basic premise of Gandhian economics, which states that "civilization in the real sense of the word consists not in the multiplication, but in the deliberate and voluntary restriction of wants."[38] Ariyaratne cites Gandhi, who said, "The essence of what I have said is that man should rest content with what are his real needs and become self-sufficient."[39] Where the present economic system creates desires that often cannot be met, Sarvodaya's village system focuses on the basic human needs. Countering hatred, the village nurtures nonviolence and sharing; countering ignorance, the village provides a context that facilitates both individual and collective awakening. Ariyaratne believes this village model would solve the problems in the six major areas of life: spiritual, moral, cultural, social, economic, and political.

Although Sarvodaya's critics may regard this vision of a village society or a Sarvodaya social order as utopian and perhaps naïve, viewed from a socially engaged Buddhist perspective, Sarvodaya's use of the vision reflects a good understanding of what is needed to build a society around humanistic and spiritual values. Sarvodaya does not seek a return to the past or to build up a Sinhala Buddhist identity; it seeks to orient society to values such as spirituality, equality, simplicity, and conservation. Sarvodaya envisions a network of village democracies where people are free to live in a way that fulfills their human potential and awakens them spiritually to pursue the Dharmic path. Well acquainted with Western civilization and its shortcomings, Ariyaratne advocates an alternative form of development that would be decentralized, people-centered, and sustainable. Sarvodaya's vision is more about "small is beautiful," than about a return to the golden age of the Anuradhapura period.

A Time of Challenge and Change

Armed with this vision of a village social revolution, Sarvodaya set out to implement it during the late 1980s and the early 1990s. In doing so, however, Sarvodaya encountered some obstacles from the government and the charitable foundations that were supporting the Movement.

In the past, Sarvodaya always tried to cooperate with the development efforts of the government and the private sector, hoping to influence them to follow Sarvodaya's vision. But during the 1980s and 1990s, what the Sarvodaya leaders already knew was confirmed: a basic difference existed between Sarvodaya's approach and that of the government and private agencies. While the government focused increasingly on top-down, macrodevelopment projects such as major irrigation systems and power-generating dams, Sarvodaya endeavored to transform the grassroots conditions in the villages. Sarvodaya became more critical of the government's economic policies, because although they were designed to alleviate poverty by bringing industrialization and modernization to the island, they actually made the situation worse.

From Sarvodaya's perspective, the macrodevelopment projects of the government and international agencies such as the World Bank failed to reach the poorest of the poor. Ariyaratne pointed to examples of this failure: "By the side of gargantuan dams are parched fields that poor farmers watch disconsolately and with mounting discontent. Under the electricity lines which carry power from the dam to the cities and factories live people who have no permanent structures to call homes and hence are not eligible for that electricity."[40] To assist these people whom the government and agencies left behind, Sarvodaya pursued a revolution that would remove the causes of poverty while mitigating the effects as well. Ariyaratne said that this is why "the Sarvodaya Movement works toward the goal of not only a no-poverty society, but also a no-affluence society . . . We believe that poverty, powerlessness, and related conditions are directly linked with affluence, imbalances, and injustices in the exercise of political and economic power and other advantages enjoyed by the few over the many. What is necessary is not a palliative, but a strategy for a total, nonviolent revolutionary transformation."[41]

In addition to clashing with the government (see following chapter) during this period, Sarvodaya also experienced a conflict of principles when it clashed with the charitable foundations supporting the Movement's work. Kantowsky described the difference between the foundation's economic approach and Sarvodaya's approach when he wrote, "Western alternatives are based on what is needed to keep those already living below the poverty line from starving. While Sarvodaya defines a maximum necessary for the well-being of all, development technocrats measure the minimum energy input required to keep individual labor intact and craving for material acquisitions growing." Sarvodaya's new goals for society were made possible "by reference to a value system that differs fundamentally from the world-view which governs modern thinking."[42] This conflict of value systems became manifest when Sarvodaya found that its international donor agencies did not share the goals of the Movement. They were more interested in providing support for economic projects or income generating projects than in Sarvodaya's social programs.

The Sarvodaya Movement went through a difficult period in the early 1990s as it struggled to balance its own vision for transforming society with the policies and demands of the foreign donor agencies and the government. Out of these difficulties, however, Sarvodaya forged its new strategy for a social revolution beginning from the village.

Administrative Challenges and the Donor Consortium

In 1986 Sarvodaya's leaders signed an agreement with Sarvodaya's five major donor foundations to set up a consortium that would regularize the funding for the Movement.[43] Previously these donors supplied money to cover most of the operating budget. After the consortium was formed, however, the donors began to demand more control over the organization. The foundations' executives who were in office at that time—as opposed to the executives during the early period—seemed to have little sympathy or understanding of Sarvodaya's philosophy of development. They attempted to push Sarvodaya in directions that were incompatible with the aims and identity of the Movement. They wanted to impose "World Bank-type financial and administrative systems," and force Sarvodaya to comply with their foundations' expectations about the meaning of development.[44] In the 1990s, this attempt to control and shape Sarvodaya resulted in a clash between what Ariyaratne viewed as the "Northern Development paradigm and the humanistic and holistic approach to development of the South."[45]

The donor consortium demanded three changes in Sarvodaya's administrative structure and its approach to development work:

1. *It argued for separating the movement aspects of Sarvodaya from the organizational aspects.* The consortium donors felt that the movement aspects involved too much emphasis on "a sense of religion" and a tendency toward politics. Using a Western model, it wanted to transform Sarvodaya from a movement into an efficient development organization. When Sarvodaya's leaders objected, saying the change conflicted with Sarvodaya' s basic philosophy and ideals, the Project Director from one donor organization replied, "We are not interested in philosophy. For us, development is a business. There is nothing idealistic about it."[46]

2. *The consortium required that Sarvodaya centralize its administration and hire professionally trained staff to lead the economic programs.* This demand contradicted Sarvodaya's basic philosophy of grassroots organization and development and its vision of a bottom-up approach to social change. Sarvodaya had endeavored to decentralize its administration and activities as far as possible. However, the consortium felt that a highly centralized system of management and financial administration was necessary to ensure that Sarvodaya's field operations were accountable. It insisted that Sarvodaya restructure its "outmoded and ineffective management structures" and commanded other changes that would bring about a top-down administrative structure.

To this point, the Movement's leadership had always been composed of people who worked their way up from the village level and totally subscribed to Sarvodaya's vision. Now the consortium insisted that Sarvodaya hire professionals in accounting, management, rural technology, and other fields, and place them in positions of leadership. These managers, who often had little understanding of what the Sarvodaya Movement was about, required high salaries that were totally incommensurate with the salaries of other Sarvodaya staff. The change in management led to morale problems, in which the original staff felt slighted, and conflicts about which programs Sarvodaya should pursue.

3. *The consortium insisted that Sarvodaya find ways to quantify development, so it could more accurately report its progress to the donor agencies.* Although Sarvodaya had from the outset defined development in qualitative terms, the consortium pressured the Movement to adopt a quantitative approach and accept quantitative measures of developmental success. Citing Sarvodaya's slogan, We build the road and the road builds us, Ariyaratne argued that the success of the kind of

development Sarvodaya sought could not be measured by material standards. The consortium, however, never concurred with this notion and now, as part of their strategy to downplay the movement elements of Sarvodaya and to emphasize the organization elements, they demanded that Sarvodaya should begin to provide quantifiable evidence of the outcome of development. In addition to making demands for quantitative changes, the consortium also insisted on more frequent assessment missions by outside monitors.

Monitors and assessors were soon descending on Sarvodaya several times a year. They had to see everything, from the records at the headquarters to the most distant fieldwork sites. During these visits all other work at Sarvodaya centers effectively ceased while the Sarvodaya officials tried to meet the demands of the monitors. This process of evaluation became so oppressive that in 1991–92, eight monitoring missions descended on Sarvodaya. Ariyaratne said, "In a less-than-two-year period as many as 123 recommendations were imposed on Sarvodaya, which were humanly impossible to implement. The senior staff of Sarvodaya had hardly any time to look at and contribute to what was happening in the villages."[47] The clash of views between Sarvodaya and the consortium was illustrated when a monitor was conducting a village site visit. When told that Sarvodaya's work in the village included a spiritual dimension, the monitor demanded to see the spirituality of the work.[48]

Although the three demands represented radical departures from Sarvodaya's philosophy and practice, Sarvodaya had to negotiate them with the donors to obtain the necessary funding for implementing its programs.

The Path to Realizing the Vision

The relations between Sarvodaya and the consortium reached a crisis in 1993 when the donors announced they planned to reduce their funding by more than 40 percent. The reduction was implemented despite the consortium's long-term commitment to Sarvodaya. As a result, Sarvodaya's leaders had to take drastic action. Sarvodaya was forced to retrench over one thousand staff members, including two-thirds of the district level staff and large numbers of the village workers. The reduction brought Sarvodaya to a standstill. District centers throughout the country that had recently been busy with activities now stood empty. Facing this financial crisis, Ariyaratne and Sarvodaya's officials were forced to reevaluate their future course.

The irony of the consortium placing demands on Sarvodaya to modify its vision of a sustainable, human-centered development program is that it was forcing Sarvodaya off its course of development at the very time when many development experts in the world development community were beginning to endorse viewpoints similar to Sarvodaya's. The United Nations Development Program's 1994 *Human Development Report*, for example, called for a "new development paradigm" that "puts people at the center of development, regards economic growth as a means and not an end . . . and respects the natural systems on which all life depends." The report went on to say that development should enable "all individuals to enlarge their human capabilities to the full and to put those capabilities to their best use in all fields—economic, social, cultural, and political."[49]

Even before the funding cuts occurred, D. A. Perera, one of the pioneer leaders of the Sarvodaya Movement, warned that the "donors have influenced the LJSSS [Sarvodaya] in many ways" and unless "there is some significant strategic change it will either collapse or survive in name only with its character significantly changed."[50] Perera suggested that, through donor influence and pressure, Sarvodaya had essentially become a delivery system for a Western idea of development rather than a movement for awakening the people and the society. Faced with this funding crisis and keenly aware of the need to return to the original ideals of the Movement, Ariyaratne declared they would simply do without donor support and return to the Movement's core goals. He told his supporters, "If we have no funding, we will restart the Movement . . . We cannot abandon our vision and organization just to please the donors."[51]

Restarting the Movement was a brilliant idea that immediately rekindled the revolutionary spirit of Sarvodaya, but was it possible? Simon Zadek observed that an organization's values are integrally related to its form, so that "it is completely inappropriate to consider the form of an organization separately from its values."[52] The form of Sarvodaya had changed considerably as it expanded, with the support of the donors, from a volunteer movement to a large NGO with a huge bureaucracy and infrastructure. Sarvodaya's values had also changed as the organization grew and responded to the suggestions and demands of the consortium. On this point, Zadek noted, "There is no doubt that the [donor] consortium had an enormous influence on the evolution of Sarvodaya."[53] Even Ariyaratne admits that, in its relations with the consortium, Sarvodaya "traded inner vitality for financial security."[54] As a result of having to negotiate its programs with the donor foundations and their monitors, both the form and the content of the Sarvodaya Movement had changed significantly. But with the partial loss of funding and the break with the donor's philosophy, Sarvodaya at least had an opportunity to regain its inner vitality and return to its own course of social reform. It was from this declaration of independence from the consortium that Sarvodaya's current programs for a village-based revolution began to be implemented.

Ten Thousand Villages and the Five Stage Village Graduation Model

In 1994, to move toward this revolution, Sarvodaya began a new initiative called the Ten Thousand Villages Development Program. Setting their sights high, Ariyaratne and the Movement projected that ten thousand or more communities of the twenty-four thousand in Sri Lanka would tread this path to the new society by the year 2001. Ariyaratne reasoned that if ten thousand villages accepted Sarvodaya's goals for social change, it would provide the critical mass necessary for a village-based social revolution that would have both economic and political implications for the country.

Sarvodaya's expansion into ten thousand villages was to be achieved by employing a Five Stage Village Graduation Model for village development. This model originally had been shaped by Sarvodaya's negotiations with the consortium, but was later continued because it served as a strategy for achieving some of Sarvodaya's basic goals.

The program was introduced in the mid-1980s when the consortium demanded accurate information and a way to audit the results of the development process. Perera explained that donors wanted to know "When are [the donors] no longer needed? When can they quit? When can [Sarvodaya] continue on its own?"[55] In order to answer these questions and to provide a yardstick for measuring village development progress, Sarvodaya invented the model. Perera wrote, "It is at this stage that [Sarvodaya] came up with its five stage model providing 'developmental mile-posts' to show more precisely the progress of the process of development. The sole purpose of this model was to satisfy the donors."[56] Ariyaratne offered a slightly different account, suggesting that this model was not invented for the donors but that Sarvodaya had been following the five stages already and put the model forward to formalize the process and satisfy the consortium's demands.[57] In any case, the consortium was pleased with the model because it provided more comprehensible and quantifiable goals for development.

The Five Stage Village Graduation Model constitutes a gradual path to village development that includes specific goals that allow villages to progress from one stage to the next. The Movement offers specific services along the way. Stage 1 involves psychological and social infrastructure development. At this initial stage Sarvodaya assists villagers in identifying local needs and organizing collectively to address these needs. To begin mobilization and create a community spirit for development, the Movement facilitates a shramadana camp in the village.

The focus on social infrastructure development is more prominent during Stage 2, in which the people are assisted in organizing the children's group, mother's group, and other core Sarvodaya groups. These groups form the base on which Sarvodaya activities and programs are built. In most villages, the mother's group and children's group are formed first, because they are associated with the founding of the Sarvodaya preschool at this stage. Sarvodaya's field workers interact with the groups, and conduct development training courses on topics such as teacher training, management training, health education, and legal aid. Village leaders are sometimes sent to Sarvodaya's headquarters for training.

Stage 3 is marked by the formation of the village-level Sarvodaya Shramadana Society. This society becomes the local branch of the larger movement. It is a legally incorporated body that can hold property and undertake projects to satisfy the basic needs of the village. The formation of the Society is a key stage in the development process, because the Movement regards it as the primary unit for local and national development. At this stage the Movement also offers technological support and assists the village in opening its own bank account.

Stages 4 and 5 represent significant steps that can be taken by the village Sarvodaya Society to become financially and spiritually independent. Stage 4 is characterized by the initiation of economic activities such as applying for loans from the Movement. Stage 4 is also marked by the start of savings and microcredit programs sponsored by the Sarvodaya Economic Enterprise Development Services unit. By Stage 5, the Society is expected to be self-managed and self-financed so it can control its own development. A Stage 5 village is also expected to assist neighboring villages who wish to begin the gradual path to development.

Working Out the Problems

The Five Stage Village Graduation Model has had a number of problems and undergone several revisions since it was devised. At first the consortium and the Sarvodaya Movement were pleased to have agreed on a system that would provide better organization and tracking of the development process. Both parties soon discovered, however, that the system was not perfect. Villages did not always move through the graduation process in a methodical way. They tended to remain at one stage longer than expected, or move backward rather than forward toward graduation. In many cases it was difficult to determine exactly which stage a village had attained. The donors' representatives complained that Sarvodaya was not monitoring the process adequately enough to provide the detailed reporting that the foundations required.[58] Sarvodaya, whose leaders knew the graduation model was somewhat theoretical, reminded the donors that the practice of development is not an exact science.

The donors, however, continued to demand a more effective application of the graduation process. They and Sarvodaya also addressed the issue of how long villages should spend at each stage. Sarvodaya later developed guidelines in an attempt to expedite the process: Stage 1 should ideally take no longer than five months to complete, Stage 2 no longer than nine months, and Stage 3 no longer than eighteen months, although in practice these stages often took much longer.[59]

In an effort to move villages through the graduation stages more efficiently, Sarvodaya, on the advice of the donors, made a decision in 1992 to reduce the number of villages in the system. The intent was to concentrate resources and assist the villages in developing more efficiently. In 1993 Sarvodaya projected that by 1994 the number of villages in each graduation stage would be as follows:

Stage 1	566
Stage 2	604
Stage 3	830
Stage 4	1,250
Stage 5	250

These numbers represented a significant reduction in Sarvodaya's desired level of village activity.[60] Perera noted that by focusing on these numbers and quotas, Sarvodaya allowed the donors to change the Movement's role from "an initiator and supporter of development" to a "producer of development."[61]

When the donors cut their funding for the Movement in 1994, Sarvodaya debated whether or not it should continue the graduation process. The field staff favored keeping the program in some form, because it provided a useful way of helping the villagers visualize the gradual development process. After considering the matter, Ariyaratne decided to retain the program in a somewhat revised form, because it contributed to Sarvodaya's goal of uniting villages horizontally and forming a "dharmic circle" that would counter the power pyramid. He viewed it as another means of empowering the people by enabling them to help each other. Ariyaratne wrote, "The current Sarvodaya strategy [for social change] is based on establishing links between communities in various stages of development so that they may support each other and also be part of a wider movement."[62]

As part of the attempt to restart the Movement, Ariyaratne decided that with some slight changes the graduation model could contribute to the new goal of reaching ten thousand villages. To do this and to emphasize the cooperative aspect of the process, Sarvodaya introduced three new categories for the villages in the graduation process: Pioneering Villages, Intermediary Villages, and Peripheral Villages. The Pioneering Villages were generally more advanced (Stages 3 to 5) and capable of providing leadership and assistance to other villages. Sarvodaya workers would assist each Pioneering Village to build up its programs, and then to form links with four neighboring Intermediary Villages and five Peripheral Villages in the beginning stages of development. In this way, each Pioneering Village would facilitate development in nine other villages. By identifying one thousand Pioneering Villages, Sarvodaya could extend the Movement to ten thousand villages, even though its budget had been cut and there were fewer professional staff working in the villages. Village volunteers would replace the hundreds of village staff or *gramadana* (field level) workers who had been laid off. In this way Sarvodaya could then empower these villages socially, economically, and technologically to build stable village structures.

This plan was consistent with Sarvodaya's ideal of sustainable, grassroots development, and reversed the centralization measures that the donors had imposed. In its most recent reports, Sarvodaya proclaims that, "As an implementation method, the Pioneering Villages Plan was an unqualified success . . . Only six districts were funded at appropriate levels during this period, and yet significant progress was made in both funded and unfunded districts."[63] From 1995 to 1998, Sarvodaya proclaimed that the Movement was active in 1,034 Pioneering Villages, 4,036 Intermediary Villages, and 6,330 Peripheral Villages for a total of eleven thousand four hundred villages, exceeding its original goal of ten thousand villages.[64]

The Economic Empowerment of the Village

Economic empowerment represents one key element introduced to the village during the graduation process. Sarvodaya's ideal of a village-based social revolution includes an economic component. However, it has never been the central goal, because Sarvodaya has sought an integrated village development and a Sarvodaya social order involving six elements: spiritual, moral, cultural, social, economic, and political. As Hans Wismeijer noted, for Sarvodaya, "development is not just an economic process, but an interplay of economic, social, religious, and psychological factors."[65] Ariyaratne wrote, "The economic life of a human being cannot be separated from his or her total life and living. . . . [The] Buddha Dhamma looks at life as a whole."[66]

Sarvodaya's perspective on economic empowerment is reflected in its list of Basic Human Needs (see page 17). As we noted, the list does not include employment or income generation as basic needs. Sarvodaya's explanation of this seeming omission is that employment and income do not represent the goals of development, but only one approach to the true goal of empowering the people. The omission of income and employment from this list of Basic Human Needs reflects Sarvodaya's interpretation of Buddhist values as the basis for its ideal social order.

Here Sarvodaya's economic views resonate with those of E. F. Schumacher, whose theories Ariyaratne respected from an early period.[67] Schumacher compared Western and Buddhist economics in this way: "The modern economist . . . is used to measuring the 'standard of living' by the amount of annual consumption, assuming all the time that a man who consumes more is 'better off' than a man who consumes less. A Buddhist economist would consider this approach excessively irrational: since consumption is merely a means to human well-being, the aim should be to obtain the maximum of well-being with the minimum of consumption."[68] He also noted that, "while the materialist is mainly interested in goods, the Buddhist is mainly interested in liberation."[69]

Sarvodaya has followed this kind of Buddhist economic development model, and projects a Sarvodaya social order that contrasts sharply with the kind of social order produced by Westernization and globalization. Whereas production-centered societies define wealth in quantitative terms and create desires for the objects that they produce, Sarvodaya declares that spiritual values represent the true wealth. Sarvodaya's model of development is "people-centered," and has as its primary aim "human awakening" rather than the creation of material

wealth. Sarvodaya aims to achieve this kind of total liberation from
what Buddhism identifies as the three systemic evils: greed, hatred, and
delusion. Goulet noted that Sarvodaya's image of awakening and development "strikes a death-blow to that 'dynamism of desire' which is the
motor-force of Western aspirations after development, capitalistic and
socialistic alike."[70] Ariyaratne argued that the "advancement of people
in a quantitative sense is meaningless and even unachievable" unless the
spiritual and qualitative factors are included also.[71] This is what Sarvodaya means by its ideal of a social order characterized by "no poverty
and no affluence."

Sarvodaya's vision of integrated development with a balance of
social, spiritual, economic, and political factors became one of the key
points of debate with the donors. Operating with a Western understanding of development that emphasizes economic progress, the donors
questioned the viability of Sarvodaya's holistic Gandhian-Buddhist
model. While the donors argued that economic progress should be given
priority, Sarvodaya contended that the economic system cannot be
changed without spiritual awakening. Sarvodaya's negotiations with the
donors on these points led to some significant transformations in the
structure of Sarvodaya's economic programs and raised questions, both
within the Movement and without, about how these transformed programs conformed to Sarvodaya's vision.

Sarvodaya Economic Enterprises Development Services

In 1987, Ariyaratne created a new program unit of Sarvodaya to deal
with the economic empowerment of the village. The unit was named
Sarvodaya Economic Enterprises Development Services (SEEDS). It was
conceived to have two missions: to help the poorer members of village
Sarvodaya societies attain a decent economic standard and to bring
some financial stability to the village. SEEDS began as a small program
that functioned within the Sarvodaya Movement and under the umbrella
of Sarvodaya's social programs. Yielding to the demands of the donors,
however, Sarvodaya elevated SEEDS to the rank of a separate division
alongside the social programs division.

This decision came as a result of the debate with the donors about
whether Sarvodaya should be a movement or an organization. The
donors wanted to separate the economic development programs from
the social and cultural development programs as part of their drive
to separate the organizational elements from the movement elements.
This kind of separation opposed Sarvodaya's basic vision of integrated
development, but conformed perfectly with the donors' ideas of how

development should proceed. The leadership of Sarvodaya went along with this plan, because the donor consortium controlled the budget at this point. However, the leaders hoped that this separation could be managed in a way that would not violate Sarvodaya's vision.

Thus, SEEDS became the comprehensive economic unit or division of Sarvodaya, with its own office and administration distinct from the central administration of Sarvodaya that oversaw the social programs. When the donors slashed their funding to the Movement in 1994, they decided to channel their reduced funding almost exclusively into the economic division. Ariyaratne has criticized the donors for creating a disparity between the economic and social programs and described this separation as a "devastating mistake that the donor consultants pushed Sarvodaya into."[72] In the period since this break with the donors, Sarvodaya has maintained the distinct status of the economic programs, but has tried to reintegrate them with the overall vision of the Movement.

Today, the Sarvodaya Movement locates economic development in the second of its three divisions, which include the Social Empowerment Division (SED), the Economic Empowerment Division, and the Technological Empowerment Division. SED, which encompasses the work of building the social and spiritual infrastructure of the village, lays the groundwork for economic development activities. The Economic Empowerment Division is led by SEEDS, which has the responsibility for three programs: the Rural Enterprise Program, the Management Training Institute, and the Rural Enterprise Development Services Program. Sarvodaya relates these economic programs to the overall vision of the Movement by regarding them as instruments for eliminating poverty and social injustice, crucial steps toward restructuring the existing social order. Sarvodaya explains that it seeks to improve the economic conditions of the poor, not as an end in itself, but as a means "to enable them to meet their basic needs, i.e., food, water, clothes, shelter, health care, and nutrition."[73] Nevertheless, economic programs remain essential to the attainment of Sarvodaya's goals; Ariyaratne believes that two of the three main problems facing the country are economic: (1.) the continued impoverishment of the bottom 60 percent of the population, (2.) the ethnic conflict, and (3.) the unreachable lifestyle being promoted by the Open Economic policies of the government.[74] Ariyaratne supports the economic programs of SEEDS, but says it "should be made to be an integral component of a human awakening programme and a sustainable programme for total awakening of human beings and society."[75]

In 1998, to move toward this kind of balance, Sarvodaya began to reassess the relationship between SED and SEEDS. The responsibilities of the two divisions were reallocated, so that SED is now primarily responsible for the development of villages up to Stage 3 and SEEDS has responsibility from Stage 3 on, when the financial programs are facilitated.

SEEDS' programs focus on establishing village banking and microcredit to alleviate poverty by encouraging grassroots enterprises and initiatives. Keying its work to the village graduation model, SEEDS works with villages that have reached Stages 3, 4, and 5. When a village has reached Stage 3 by establishing the basic social infrastructure and starting its Early Childhood Education program and preschool, Sarvodaya introduces the Rural Enterprise Program (REP). REP assists villagers with setting up a savings section that can also give small loans to Sarvodaya Society members. REP's mission is "to make a sustainable increase in the income levels of the poorer members of Sarvodaya village societies" and to enable these societies to fund their own development activities.

The other two SEEDS programs support the economic empowerment work of REP. The Management Training Institute conducts various kinds of educational programs designed to teach villagers how to manage and finance their agricultural and small business enterprises. The Rural Enterprises Development Services (REDS) program provides extension services in the areas of agriculture and small business development. The goal of REDS is to ensure that villagers who start projects with microcredit get the help and advice they need to be successful.

A Closer Look at SEEDS' Savings and Microcredit Programs

Sarvodaya decided to begin village savings and microcredit programs, because it found that the commercial banks did not have the kind of long-term vision necessary to assist the poor. Commercial banks in Sri Lanka, like commercial banks in most places, were only interested in making reliable loans that would safely earn a profit. To fill the need and empower the rural poor economically, SEEDS began establishing savings and credit sections in villages having a Sarvodaya Society. In such villages, SEEDS recruits local leaders and office bearers to form an economic subcommittee to oversee the village savings section and approve loan applications. To apply for a loan, a person must be an active member of a village Sarvodaya Society and have a savings account with the Sarvodaya savings section or bank. When a village Sarvodaya Society reaches Stage 5 and its savings section attains a certain level of deposits, it can apply to become a village bank. Savings sections can give small loans of about Rs 2000, but village banks can give much larger loans depending on the deposits of the bank.

By 1999, SEEDS had facilitated the establishment of savings sections in over two thousand villages; in two hundred and eight of these villages it had helped the villagers set up village banks. Jude Fernando notes that in 1994–95, the total savings in Sarvodaya Societies amounted to Rs 64.4 million and the total loans came to Rs 375 million. The sources of the loan funds were: Rs 38 million from the government's Janasaviya Trust Fund; Rs 219.7 million from the Sarvodaya revolving fund; Rs 105.4 million from village savings; and Rs 12.1 million from commercial banks.[76] In 1996–97, the SEEDS savings sections and banks reported total savings of Rs 159.7 million and total loans of Rs 887 million.[77]

In the first few years, SEEDS banks and savings sections had a poor repayment rate, because their borrowers experienced many business failures. This situation was corrected by setting up REDS to provide extension services to the local entrepreneurs who took out the loans. Now SEEDS banks have a very good repayment rate, which, the director of SEEDS explains, also is a function of the Sarvodaya culture of discipline and honesty.[78] In 1996–97, the repayment rate was 90 percent and in 2000 the repayment rate was 93 percent. Looking to the future, SEEDS plans to develop the banking program in two ways. First, it proposes decentralizing an increasing amount of the management and decision making to the village societies. And, second, it plans to establish a Sarvodaya Development Bank that will be a self-sustaining parent body for all of the village banks and savings societies.

How successful have these SEEDS banking programs been in empowering the poor? There is no doubt that the village savings sections and banks have been well received by the people, who feel they provide more accessible financial services at the village level. Villagers explain that before the Sarvodaya bank opened in their village, they had to go to the nearest large town or to the government rural bank to apply for loans. This process usually took time and entailed a considerable amount of red tape in the form of applications, references, and other hurdles. The only alternative to large town and government banks was the local money lender, who typically charged a very high rate of interest for small loans.

The Sarvodaya bank or savings section provides a much more people-friendly approach to these matters. The bank is usually located in a village house, and the loans are approved by a committee of village neighbors. Instead of setting up barriers that discourage people from applying for loans, Sarvodaya encourages people to apply and offers loan rates that are much lower than those of the commercial banks.

Sarvodaya does not insist on collateral for small loans, and provides extension services to help people succeed with the projects they are financing. Sarvodaya also encourages members to open savings accounts in the local savings section. One obvious advantage of these savings sections and banks is that the villagers' funds remain in the village, rather than deposited in a bank in the city, and serve as a base for the loans that empower the local community.

Sarvodaya reported that from 1987 to 1989, some thirty-four thousand villagers received loans from SEEDS savings programs, and an estimated five thousand six hundred villagers became self-employed with these loans.[79] In 2000–01, 204,751 people received loans of various kinds from Sarvodaya, totaling Rs 908.2 million.[80] Some purposes for which Sarvodaya loans funds include agriculture, trade, cottage industry, livestock, and services.[81]

In visits to Sarvodaya villages, I met some of the people who have benefited from the Sarvodaya economic activities, and saw some of the projects supported by SEEDS loans. In one village, for example, SEEDS loans have made a small bakery, several small food shops, a tea shop, a cottage industry where women make bags and backpacks, a woodworking shop, and a small dairy possible. Some of these businesses are run by people who were previously employed in Colombo, but decided to return to their village and start their own businesses. A large percentage of Sarvodaya's loans for entrepreneurial activities go to women. In 1998, 63 percent of these loans went to women who then started shops and businesses that have become very successful. One woman said the loan she received from the Sarvodaya bank facilitated her success with her small store. When I asked what was the most important contribution Sarvodaya has made to the village, most people I spoke to identified the banking scheme as having the greatest benefit.[82]

SEEDS' Contribution to the Sarvodaya Vision

While it seems clear that the SEEDS programs have been fairly successful in a financial sense, one could ask to what extent they have advanced the Sarvodaya vision, especially after the break with the donors. To put the question another way, do these programs represent socially engaged Buddhism or simply a form of village economic development that could be done by any development agency? The director of SEEDS, Saliyah Ranasinghe, stressed the close relationship between the economic programs and the social programs of the Sarvodaya Movement. The social programs lay a foundation for the economic and technological programs in the village. In return, these financial programs benefit both the Sarvodaya Movement and the social programs by strengthening the village Sarvodaya Societies and attracting new members.

Critics of Sarvodaya, however, have expressed doubts about this function of the economic programs. A former meditation teacher said he thought the loan program caused people to regard Sarvodaya as "just another way to make a buck" and to miss the spiritual content of the Movement. Other critics argued that the financial programs distract people from the purpose of Sarvodaya and often become the main reason why villagers form Sarvodaya Societies. Fernando, in his comparative study of the banking program, found that "the introduction of microcredit has somewhat increased the people's interest in the activities of the movement." But he also found that participation in the village societies of the Anuradhapura district was still quite low.[83]

Despite the views of some critics, Sarvodaya's annual reports show that both the participation in the Movement and the figures for the banking programs have increased steadily in recent years. This seems to indicate that the programs are meeting one of Sarvodaya's goals: the empowerment of the village and the poor. Ariyaratne said, "At the village level, one of the main factors contributing to the elimination of poverty is the encouragement of savings."[84]

The chairman of a Sarvodaya village society discussed the question of whether this kind of economic development conforms to Sarvodaya's vision. He said that, through its financial programs, Sarvodaya promotes a form of Buddhist development that is good for the village. For example, he noted that the dairy program in his village that was started with a loan from Sarvodaya provides income and food, but it does not involve killing animals. Sarvodaya would not give loans for raising pigs, hens, or goats, he said, because these animals would be killed for consumption. He also observed that the SEEDS programs encourage villagers to improve themselves and help them to overcome feelings that it may be somehow improper for Buddhists to have ambition. Sarvodaya teaches them that it is not against Buddhism to take initiative to improve oneself and one's village. He also noted that since the Sarvodaya's programs began in his village, there has been more unity and pride.[85]

The leaders of Sarvodaya regard Sarvodaya's economic programs as integral to the Movement's goals. Ranasinghe explained that the village banks foster an updated version of the Gandhian vision of development. He noted that Gandhi promoted the spinning wheel and, although that ideal is not viable now, village entrepreneurs and cottage industries represent

a contemporary expression of it. In his view, the open economy has created opportunities for people in the village who can use Sarvodaya's
microcredit to start businesses that are needed. Explaining that in this
economy even villages are market driven, he said SEEDS programs help
people understand and cope with the market.[86] Although Ranasinghe
made reference to Gandhi and spoke of the importance of "barefoot
bankers," his basic perspective on development seems somewhat Western, with its emphasis on entrepreneurs and the open economy.

Ariyaratne, on the other hand, explains these economic programs in
a much more revolutionary way, as expressions of Sarvodaya's Gandhian-
Buddhist ideal. He regards these programs not so much as ways to
enable villagers to fit into the current open economy, but as the foundation for a comprehensive social revolution that will bring an alternative
economic structure. Ariyaratne compares Sarvodaya's recent economic
programs to Gandhi's Constructive Program.

In his essay on the Constructive Program, Gandhi emphasized the
connection between village, social, and economic reforms and the goal
of independence through a nonviolent revolution. Gandhi observed,
"The constructive programme may otherwise and more fittingly be
called construction of *poorna swaraj* or complete independence by
truthful and nonviolent means." [87] As Kantowsky notes, for Gandhi the
Constructive Program was "central to the understanding of Gandhi's
concept of *Swaraj,* which was for him a step towards the goal of 'Ram
Raj,' the Kingdom of God, where an equal share was given 'even unto
this last'."[88]

The Right Livelihood Society: An Experiment

Ariyaratne clearly follows Gandhi by regarding the economic programs
as closely linked to the Sarvodaya ideal of a nonviolent social revolution
at the grassroots level.

Comparing Gandhi's idea of gram swaraj with the Buddhist teachings
on Right Livelihood, Ariyaratne noted that "this experiment including
the economic and political aspects is going on in some 2500 advanced
villages."[89] Ariyaratne described the alternative socioeconomic structure
that is the focus of this "experiment" as a Right Livelihood society or
"full engagement society." In his view, a Right Livelihood society would
facilitate "the engagement of each and every individual in socially
acceptable and useful activities (constructive activities) which also give
them a sense of satisfaction."[90] This is Ariyaratne's Buddhist interpretation of Gandhi's ideal of a society "where an equal share is given 'even
unto this last.'"[91]

Ariyaratne used the idea of the Right Livelihood society to critique Western and global economic models that focus on income and employment. He summarized the nature of his break with Western economies in this statement:

> "We should rethink the validity or feasibility of blindly following the Western economic theory and practice. Perhaps a theory of a full engagement society will be a more feasible and realizable concept in our rural situations. Gandhiji talked about production by the masses rather than mass production . . . Lord Buddha included Right Livelihood in his Noble Eightfold Path. Dr. E. F. Schumacher introduced Buddhist Economics in his famous book, *Small is Beautiful*. Now the time has come to experiment with these ideas and concepts."[92]

In Ariyaratne's view, free market economies do not lead to the satisfaction of basic human needs, but instead create unrealizable desires. He argued that "Sarvodaya has demonstrated that the full engagement of all in the community can lead to the satisfaction of basic human needs even in the absence of full employment as economists conceive it."[93] In his view of a "full engagement society," Ariyaratne is charting a course that clearly goes beyond the present economic programs. He hopes the current programs can lead to the kind of village economy in which everyone can contribute and share. In moving toward this economy, Sarvodaya is preparing the villages to be self-reliant and participate in a "Dharmic circle" of villages that can buffer the pressures and uncertainties of the national and global economies. Ariyaratne looks to the economic programs to "organize the production, distribution, and consumption in the Sarvodaya villages and village clusters . . . so that they could effectively confront the onslaughts of the violent and capitalist commercial economy invading them from without and to build an economic cover through that to protect the common man."[94] Although Ariyaratne's vision here runs ahead of that of SEEDS, and probably the vision of the average Sarvodaya member who participates in the village economic programs, his idealism is central to the Movement's goal of building an alternative economy that will both survive and supersede the current economy.

An interesting example of Ariyaratne's belief in this new economy and a pending revolution occurred when he spoke to the students at a high school in Mahiyangana, Sri Lanka in 1997. In his address he dealt with the question of the meaning of education. He said that, although the World Bank has defined education as primarily a means to employment, real education must be much broader than this. Education, Ariyaratne said, should prepare one for life. He was not sure, he went on, that their education should necessarily prepare them to go to the city and get jobs in the present system, because that may not represent the best option for them. Looking to the future, he said, an alternative system is emerging, which will be quite different from the present economic system. The new system will be a holistic, grassroots system that includes all people and leaves no one behind. It is for this holistic system that their education should prepare them. This new economic system will lead to the awakening of all and to the total, nonviolent revolution for which Sarvodaya has been laying the groundwork.

CHAPTER FOUR

SARVODAYA AND THE POLITICAL EMPOWERMENT OF THE VILLAGE*

The political empowerment of the village represents the third pillar of Sarvodaya's social revolution, alongside economic empowerment and social transformation. Sarvodaya's attitude toward and relations with the government of Sri Lanka and the present political system has evolved since the Movement's beginning, but reached a critical point in the late 1980s. From the beginning of the Movement, Sarvodaya has had reservations about the party political system, reservations that stem from Sarvodaya's ties to the views of Gandhi and Vinoba Bhave in India. Vinoba said, for example, "Political parties detract one from self-less service. They create all sorts of differences, they divide people in water-tight compartments."[1]

Writing as early as 1961, Ariyaratne similarly criticized the system of party politics that Sri Lanka inherited from the British. He said no one thought about developing "a system of government which suited our environment and was capable of leading to the realization of our national objectives." Ariyaratne went on to explain, however, that "the shramadana movement was started to make good this basic deficiency and to create a people's strength (*janashakti* or *janasaviya*) which, without party affiliations, would be powerful enough to bring together into one front all citizens for the common social and economic progress of the country."[2] Similarly, in 1974, Ariyaratne described the Sarvodaya Movement as rejecting the current political system. He said, "We do not align ourselves with political parties or power blocks, but try to build up enlightened people's action from below as the fastest and most effective means our contemporary society has for rapid social change."[3]

Sarvodaya's goal from the outset was described by Ariyaratne as "a dynamic nonviolent revolution which is not a transfer of political, economic, or social power from one party or class to another, but the transfer of all such power to the people."[4] But despite these statements about their distrust of the existing party political system and their hopes for a social revolution, Sarvodaya has followed a strategy of cooperating with the government, rather than opposing it, during most of its history. This approach worked well for Sarvodaya until the ethnic conflict erupted in 1983 and the nation became engulfed by the conflict in the following years. At that point, Sarvodaya was forced to adopt a more revolutionary strategy that sought to actualize its ideal of an alternative political system.

Sarvodaya's Strategy of Cooperation with the Government

The Sarvodaya Movement adopted an optimistic and pragmatic attitude of tolerance toward the ruling governments until the mid-1980s. In 1978, Ariyaratne justified this attitude by saying, "When some aspects of the established order conform with the righteous principles of the Movement, the Movement cooperates with those aspects. When they become unrighteous . . . the Movement does not cooperate and may even extend nonviolent non-cooperation."[5]

Detlef Kantowsky compared Sarvodaya in Sri Lanka with the Indian Sarvodaya movement on this point, showing that the Sri Lankan movement followed the paradigm of the righteous ruler that came from Buddhist sources. He wrote,

> "Sarvodaya's work in Sri Lanka and its cooperation with the government is supported by a Buddhist theory of a welfare-state that Hindu political history lacks. . . . Sarvodaya in Sri Lanka hopes that rules of the Dharma will regain control over the minds of men, so that the rulers will be righteous and provide the . . . kinds of infrastructure necessary for the well-being of their citizens."[6]

Goulet, writing in 1981, similarly argued that Sarvodaya had a philosophical reason for its selective cooperation with the government. "The philosophical principle at issue is the Buddhist vision of a Dharmic or righteous society which requires all citizens and even the Sangha (Order) of monks to summon, to recall, and to stimulate their rulers to practice justice and equity in their governance of society."[7]

Whereas, as Kantowsky pointed out, Gandhi's political system more or less anticipated the "abolition of the state," Ariyaratne believed that the state could be made righteous and that the ruler had a responsibility to follow the Dharma.[8] In Sarvodaya writings, Ariyaratne argued that "a ruler must comply with the ten royal virtues of the highest level"[9] and that

> "the vision of traditional morality, like a continuous unbroken string has influenced the rulers [of Sri Lanka] down the ages. Hence the rulers have had to grapple with the dilemma of reconciling the qualities of the righteous ruler derived from Buddhist political theory with the needs of everyday political management."[10]

Commenting on these views, Goulet noted, "Although Sarvodayans understand that governments come and go, that development models ebb and rise, they are not anarchists; nor are they radically opposed to states or governments."[11] Sarvodaya advocated social revolution, but it took a gradualist approach to it and believed that the government could be influenced to follow the path to a dharmic social revolution. In this attitude they were also following a Gandhian model to some extent. Hans Wismeijer points out that Indian Sarvodayans also had some anarchistic tendencies, but they were gradualists too, believing that "the anarchist goal can only be reached after man has reached a higher spiritual level."[12]

This mood of optimistic, dharmic cooperation certainly seems to have characterized Sarvodaya's attitude toward the government in 1977, when the United National Party (UNP) government of President J. R. Jayawardene took office. Sarvodaya had had cordial relations with the regime of Jayawardene's predecessor, Sirimavo Bandaranaike, although the Home Minister in her government, Felix Bandaranaike, had openly opposed the movement.[13] When Jayawardene was elected, however, Sarvodaya began to feel that it could expand its programs in the country and assume a national role by cooperating with the new government.

Sarvodaya was drawn to Jayawardene, in part because he was a strong supporter of Buddhism. Jayawardene and the UNP came to power promising to establish a *dharmiṣṭha* society, a society based on the principles of the Buddha's Dharma. Jayawardene said, "The U.N.P. government aims at building a new society on the foundation of the principles of Buddha Dharma. We have a duty to protect the Buddha *sāsana* (teaching) and to pledge that every possible action will be taken to develop it."[14]

Jayawardene was following the same pattern as other Sri Lankan governments since independence: They appealed to the legends from the *Mahāvamsa,* the Chronicle of Sri Lanka, as the basis for the "manifest destiny" of the Sinhalese to be the guardians of the Dharma. For these governments, this legacy provided a mandate that supported the Buddhist identity of the people as well as the government. Although these Sinhala Buddhist regimes stopped just short of making Buddhism the state religion, they made it clear that it was the duty of the state to accord Buddhism "the foremost place," while protecting and fostering all other religions also.

While emphasizing their Buddhist identity, these governments also employed a rhetoric that extolled Buddhist values, such as compassion and nonviolence. As time went on, however, it became evident that these two ideals existed in tension: The more the Sinhalese Buddhists asserted and supported their Buddhist identity, the more they created an "other" of the Tamil minority toward whom it became increasingly difficult to show compassion and nonviolence. The pro-Sinhala policies of the government contributed initially to the alienation of the Tamil minority and ultimately to the Tamil separatist movement. But at the beginning, Sarvodaya did not foresee this; it saw only that Jayawardene appeared to fulfill the role of a Buddhist ruler who followed the Ten Royal Virtues (*dasa rāja dhammā*).

A Relationship of Opportunity and Risk

In March 1978, President Jayawardene was the "chief guest" at the dedication ceremony for Sarvodaya's new headquarters complex in Moratuwa. In his speech on that occasion he said, "Our government and the Sarvodaya Movement have many things in common. Both endeavor to create a peaceful, righteous, and prosperous society in Sri Lanka based on the teachings embodied in the *Dhamma Chakka Sutta* of the Buddha."[15] A month later, the new Prime Minister R. Premadasa, speaking at a conference on "Sarvodaya and Development," elaborated on the prospect of the government and Sarvodaya working closely together to achieve their goals. He said, "The government has decided to enlist the support of the Sarvodaya Movement to build the righteous society it envisages. . . . The Sarvodaya Movement will be made use of by local authorities to serve the people."[16] Ariyaratne and the Sarvodaya leaders felt that the strategy of cooperation would give the Movement increased influence and credibility.

Ariyaratne said, "The active participation of two Prime Ministers and the first elected Executive President of the Republic of Sri Lanka in important Sarvodaya events has further established the bona fides of the Movement in the minds of the people."[17]

Building on this momentum, Sarvodaya drew up a five-year plan, to begin in 1978, to devise ways "to harmonize and work in close cooperation with the national development effort of the government of Sri Lanka."[18] In the next few years, Sarvodaya and the government worked together on a number of projects related to development. Sarvodaya conducted training sessions and special orientations for government officials to teach them about Sarvodaya's approach to development. The Movement also assisted the government in its efforts to improve rural schools in the poorest villages.[19] Premadasa enlisted Ariyaratne's help in devising a scheme for revitalizing the most impoverished villages. He called it *gamudawa* and patterned it after Sarvodaya's system of gramodaya. For a number of years, Ariyaratne served as a consultant to this program and regularly participated in the grand openings of the elaborately reconstructed gamudawa villages. He said, "The Sarvodaya Shramadana Movement actively participates in this scheme in every possible respect. These new developments have opened new possibilities for carrying the Sarvodaya message to a wider population."[20] As Prime Minister, Premadasa continued to encourage Sarvodaya, saying, "I have no doubt that before long the whole country, all the people of this country, will get themselves inspired and motivated by Sarvodaya to work selflessly for the cause of humanity."[21]

If cooperation with the government presented new opportunities for Sarvodaya to enter the national stage and expand its work, it also presented new risks that the Movement would be regarded as political and identified with the elite power brokers. Ariyaratne realized this in 1982 when he wrote about a "struggle to awaken without acquiescence."[22] In explaining how the Movement could maintain its integrity and its own goals while working closely with the government, he noted, "Sarvodaya does not consider that confrontation with the government is the only path to the liberation of people and to the progress of the nation."[23] He thought that Sarvodaya could ride the tiger of government cooperation and still further its own agenda. He reasoned that, "If a people's movement, because of its integrity and record of service and its adherence to a code of ethics approved by the people can command the respect of the government, such a movement can undoubtedly influence the government to bring about accelerated social change, nonviolently. Our relationship with the present government is determined by this principle."[24]

Wismeijer surveyed the Sarvodaya leadership during this period and found they agreed in general with the strategy of cooperation with the government. But they also had some serious concerns about this policy. When asked if "the movement should pay more attention to the government's development programmes as a means of achieving Sarvodaya society," a majority of Wismeijer's respondents agreed with this idea (61 percent in favor, 32 percent against). However, when asked if they thought Sarvodaya members should assist political candidates who either had supported Sarvodaya or would support Sarvodaya in the future, the majority responded that it was not wise to be drawn into party politics for whatever reason. Further, Wismeijer asked if they thought that "by working together with government institutions the movement is in danger of losing its impartiality." To this question, the leaders were divided: 47 percent disagreed but 46.7 percent agreed. This shows, as Wismeijer noted, that a significant number of Sarvodaya leaders who were on the frontlines of Sarvodaya's work in society were concerned that Sarvodaya could lose its apolitical nature or its "impartiality, which is an important item of the movement's ideology."[25]

Outside observers at the time had similar concerns about Sarvodaya losing its identity. Kantowsky suggested, "Sarvodaya is now, at the end of 1978, probably just on the brink of being corrupted . . . The United National Party (UNP), now in power, tries to use Sarvodaya's image of traditional righteousness to camouflage modernization strategies that obviously run counter to basic tendencies of the Movement."[26]

Although Jayawardene spoke about establishing a dharmic government, his implementation of that ideal turned out to be quite different from Sarvodaya's vision of a dharmic state. For example, although he frequently invoked the ideal of the Emperor Asoka, Jayawardene did not acknowledge that the Dharma had implications for the social and economic policymaking of a modern government. Both the UNP and Jayawardene were committed to fostering a capitalist, free-market economy that would produce prosperity for the country. Kemper notes that Jayawardene saw no conflict between these goals and Buddhism, because he understood Buddhism to be primarily a religion of personal morality and individual responsibility.[27] Clearly these policies ran counter to the principles of the Sarvodaya Movement, but Sarvodaya remained optimistic about being able to instruct the government. Reflecting a confidence in the new UNP government, Ariyaratne said, "Today there appears to be general acceptance on the part of the politicians who cherish ethical principles that Sarvodaya is a much needed people's political awakening process that may do good to the people and also contribute to bring sanity into politics."[28]

Sarvodaya's version of engaged Buddhist sanity proved difficult to establish in the UNP however, as Jayawardene continued on his path of nationalistic, capitalistic, and individualistic Buddhism. The Sinhala Buddhists who elected him appeared to be impressed with his elaborate displays of merit-making, such as sponsoring the lighting of eighty-four thousand oil lamps at the Buddhist shrines.[29] These supporters did not seem concerned that, although Jayawardene participated in these public affirmations of Buddhism, he refused to enact policies and laws that would enforce Buddhist values. Even when socially engaged Buddhists appealed to the government to ban the slaughter of animals or the production and sale of liquor, Jayawardene refused to support such legislation. To him, Buddhism was a personal matter and should be kept separate from government policy formation, even in a dharmistha state.

Jayawardene's perspective on Buddhism and government stemmed from his background as a member of the English-educated elite that inherited power from the British. His generation of leaders had been trained to believe that the achievement of modernization and progress in both society and government required one to devalue the role of religion. Traditional societies were characterized, and often dominated so this theory held, by religion. Therefore, to build a modern society, political leaders had to diminish the pervasive influence of religion and move toward secularization. Applying this kind of modernization and secularization theory while maintaining that one was establishing a dharmistha state might seem difficult; but Jayawardene's view that religion is only a matter of personal responsibility enabled him to keep the political and religious realms separate, in much the same way that conservative politicians have in the West.

Goulet reported that, in the first years of Jayawardene's government, Ariyaratne "dismissed as trivial the charge that many Sri Lankan urban professionals and elites perceived the movement's collaboration with the present government as compromising it."[30] Kantowsky observed prophetically that Sarvodaya in Sri Lanka had reached the same level of integration with the government that the Indian Sarvodaya movement reached in the late sixties. He said that it was possible that Sarvodaya in Sri Lanka "will also be drawn into a conflict with the government under the banner of 'Total Revolution' if it wants to keep to its principles." Kantowsky said that such a clash with the government might happen, but thought that "neither the Movement's concept of personality nor its concept of state is a pointer in that direction."[31] He did not, however, foresee the possibility that the Movement's commitment to the Gandhian ideal of nonviolence and its disagreement with the UNP's economic policies would cause just such a break with the government.

Sarvodaya's Break with the Government

Sarvodaya's optimism about being able to work with Jayawardene's government to build a dharmic nation eroded quickly after the riots of July 1983 and the escalation of the ethnic conflict in the north and east. In the turbulent years after 1983, Sarvodaya was forced to sever its ties with the government and adopt a new strategy in order to implement its own alternative vision of revolution in the political and economic realms. To some extent, Sarvodaya's views were shaped in response to the dominant discourse of this period in Sri Lanka, which was increasingly critical of Jayawardene and his policies. A chief difference between Sarvodaya and the dominant discourse was that, although others were calling for a militant and violent solution, Sarvodaya remained true to its alternative vision of a nonviolent revolution.

The two most vocal groups shaping the dominant discourse were the Sangha and the Janatha Vimukti Peramuna (JVP). From 1983 on, leading voices in the Sangha demanded that Jayawardene solve the "terrorism" problem in the north by using military force to quell the rebels. In a 1984 meeting, the Venerable Dr. Walpola Rahula, who had been a supporter of Jayawardene, criticized the government and called for Jayawardene to "eradicate terrorism militarily."[32] Jayawardene seems to have initially opposed a military solution and the use of violence to counter the rebels, but the Sangha and other groups continued to pressure him. This pressure intensified after the Liberation Tigers of Tamil Eelam (LTTE) staged two vicious attacks in 1985 and 1986. In the first attack, the LTTE infiltrated the precincts of the Buddhist shrine of the sacred Bo Tree at Anuradhapura, and then massacred and wounded hundreds of innocent Buddhists who were worshiping there. The following year, the LTTE stopped a school bus and killed a group of young Buddhist monks and students. In the wake of these two terrible events, leading monks labeled Jayawardene a traitor and insisted that he resign. The Venerable M. Sobhita blamed the government for "the river of blood" that had flowed in Anuradhapura, and demanded that "the government must resign without destroying the country and the nation."[33]

The crisis deepened in July 1987 when Jayawardene signed the Indo-Sri Lanka Peace Accord which allowed for the Indian army to enter Sri Lanka to combat the LTTE. The presence of Indian troops on Sri Lankan soil fueled demonstrations from the Sangha and the newly reborn JVP. The Sangha took to the streets to protest, and the JVP accused Jayawardene of being a "traitor." Even newspaper articles from the normally pro-government press declared that the Peace Accord represented "the biggest treason the government has committed against Buddhism."[34]

Although Jayawardene banned the JVP, it grew rapidly as an underground movement that had both influence and power in the country. The JVP launched a crusade to liberate the country from both Jayawardene's government and the Indian Peace Keeping Force (IPKF), which they sarcastically referred to as the "Indian People Killing Force." Employing tactics of terror and violence, the JVP gained de facto control of many areas of the country. It assassinated many of its opponents and attempted to assassinate Jayawardene. Many students, including young monks, formed an important part of the JVP's constituency. Abeysekara reported, "By the late 1980s the majority of the monastic student population at all universities had joined the JVP."[35] Rohan Gunaratna described the situation in 1988 as one where the JVP had become "the unseen government which ran the country. A state of near anarchy prevailed."[36]

It was in this volatile context that Ariyaratne issued his treatise, *The Power Pyramid and the Dharmic Cycle*. The book signaled the Movement's disenchantment with Jayawardene and expressed partial solidarity with those who were calling for change. Although a few years earlier Sarvodaya had had high hopes of working with the government to apply Buddhist principles to social problems, now Ariyaratne blamed the government for continuing the postcolonial trend in Sri Lanka of "abandoning the Buddhist-Hindu pattern of living that had prevailed for over two thousand five hundred years" and following "a Western, materialistic, evil, counter-cultural pattern of living."[37] Although he had expected the government to live up to the Buddhist ideals for a ruler, he now said that the political and economic policies of the government "can hardly be called Buddhist either in precept or practice."[38]

Ariyaratne expressed his general disillusionment with the failure of all politicians since independence to implement the Buddhist ideals that reformers such as Dharmapāla had lifted up. "It is the misfortune of the nation that after Mr. Bandaranaike there has not emerged in the field of politics any leadership that has had an understanding of the local thinking and culture to enable it to advance the revolution in thinking that took place in 1956."[39] Ariyaratne also argued that Bandaranaike would have united the Tamil, Christian, and Muslim minorities if the "short sighted Sinhala Buddhist leaders" had not put obstacles in his way.[40]

Ariyaratne's critique of the government focused on several points, including the party political system, the economy, and especially the use of violence. With regard to political parties, he wrote, "This system of party politics which does not accord with our values and which destroys our local thinking has been responsible not so much for the development of our country as for the ruining of it."[41] As the previous chapter illustrated, Sarvodaya rejected the economic policies that the Jayawardene government was pursuing. Ariyaratne realized that the open economy ran counter to Sarvodaya's goal of uplifting the poorest of the poor. He objected to the way the government was promoting materialism and he argued that consumerism went against the Buddha's teachings. Above all, Ariyaratne disagreed with the government's use of violence. He critiqued the Jayawardene government, writing that it had "reached a helpless stage where the law of force is in operation rather than the force of law."[42] He recognized that violence had become pervasive in the society because of government policies. "One does not require explanatory treatises to realise that the prevailing social system is a violent oppressive system . . . what we have today is not only the perpetration of individual oppression. In economic, political and various social establishments, violence has become institutionalised."[43]

Ariyaratne also expressed sympathy for the young people in the north and the south who had adopted violence to counter the government.[44] He saw their revolt as a reaction to the government's institutionalized violence. Going against the dominant discourse from both the JVP and the LTTE, Ariyaratne argued that neither the violence nor the counterviolence represented the solution. What was needed, he declared, was the kind of revolution "that can only happen through nonviolent and creative means; only by the awakening of the minds of the people through broad and democratic people's participation."[45] Toward this end he declared that he wrote *The Power Pyramid and the Dharmic Cycle* as a manifesto to show how the "Path of Sarvodaya" might rescue "this nation from the jaws of destruction."[46]

Premadasa's Approach to the Presidency

When Prime Minister R. Premadasa succeeded Jayawardene as president in December of 1988, Sarvodaya's hopes for renewed cooperation with the government to achieve a Sarvodaya social order were briefly raised, only to be quickly dashed when the new president launched an all-out attack on the Sarvodaya Movement. At the outset, the prospects looked favorable for Sarvodaya to be able to collaborate with Premadasa, because he came to power as a strong supporter of Buddhism and had close ties to Ariyaratne and the Movement. He had enlisted Ariyaratne's help with his gamudawa program, and had appeared at many Sarvodaya events during his term as Prime Minister. Premadasa also opposed the Peace Accord, and promised to resolve the intrusion of the IPKF: both policies that seemed likely to lessen the level of violence.

When he was campaigning for the presidency, Premadasa had invited Ariyaratne to join his campaign. Ariyaratne, however, refused the invitation, primarily because he wanted to adhere to Sarvodaya's longstanding policy of staying aloof from party politics. Since Premadasa had had such close contact with Sarvodaya, one might have expected that he would respect Ariyaratne's reasons for not joining his campaign. Instead, he chose to interpret Ariyaratne's refusal as opposition to his campaign and began to view Ariyaratne and his Movement with suspicion.

Although Premadasa was a pious Buddhist, his interpretation of Buddhism was in many ways much more dangerous—for the country and ultimately for Sarvodaya—than that of Jayawardene. Premadasa did not share the commitment to keeping the government secular that Jayawardene and previous leaders since independence had. Premadasa explicitly said that he did not "believe in the policy that the administration of the government and religions or the spiritual well-being of the people are separate things and should be divorced from one another. If King Dharmasoka was able to infuse Dhamma and spiritualism into the administrative set up, why cannot we achieve it? We can certainly pursue such a policy."[47]

Premadasa endeavored to link his role as head of state with that of the ancient and ideal Buddhist kings, such as Asoka, much more explicitly than his predecessors had. According to the ancient Chronicles of Sri Lanka, the ideal kings exercised two important and related functions: They were the supreme devotees and patrons of Buddhism and they were active defenders of Buddhism even using force when necessary to protect the Dharma. Josine van der Horst noted that Premadasa seems to have been drawn to the image of Asoka as a righteous king who had been involved with violence, and who continued to exercise force to protect the Dharma.[48] She argued that Premadasa's aspirations to be regarded as this kind of ideal Buddhist king led to his personally holding the portfolios of both the Ministry of Buddha Sāsana and the Ministry of Defense.[49] Premadasa identified himself as both the spiritual and the military leader of the people; and, as he understood, both of these roles were to be involved with the government's duty to support Buddhism. In his inaugural address for the new Ministry of Buddha Sāsana that he established, Premadasa declared that he would follow Asoka in carrying out a campaign of *Dharmavijaya* (conquest by Dharma).

Throughout Premadasa's time in office, the country was barraged with examples of the president's patronage of Buddhism. The government-controlled press and media carried daily stories about the president's appearances at various Buddhist ceremonies and his presentations of gifts to large and small Buddhist temples. He sponsored and participated in countless *Bodhi pūjā* (bodhi tree veneration) and almsgivings; he presented temples with golden Buddha statues and he renovated ancient Buddhist shrines. To be sure, the president also supported the other religions of the country, but this also helped him play the role of a modern-day Asoka who, according to the Chronicles, patronized all of the religions in his realm. Although Premadasa was considerably more energetic than Jayawardene in his participation in and support of Buddhism, the nature of his practice reveals that he understood Buddhism in much the same way as his predecessor. For both, Buddhism was a religion of individual morality and merit-making. By sponsoring enormous alms-giving ceremonies, such as the one that he organized in Kandy for three thousand handicapped persons, Premadasa demonstrated to the public how great the merit he was accumulating was. To show his adherence to Buddhist morality, he made it known that he followed a strict Buddhist lifestyle that prohibited excesses such as the use of tobacco or alcohol.

Premadasa's zealous support of the rituals and institutions of Buddhism related directly to the other aspect of the royal identity he aspired to: the protection and defense of Buddhism. This proved to be an ironic role for Premadasa, because he was forced to oppose the JVP, who were aligned with many factions of the Sangha. Premadasa employed massive force to crush the JVP during 1989 and 1990. The violent force with which Premadasa's army and secret police smashed the JVP caused many people to question Premadasa's claim to be following the pattern of an ideal Buddhist ruler. For his part, however, Premadasa seems to have believed that his use of violence represented an aspect of his kinship with Asoka. As van der Horst observed, "Premadasa's Asokan ideology with its particular interpretation of *Cakkavatti* kingship following the procedure of peace after conquest provides a new framework which —being well-embedded in the cultural habitus—Premadasa hopes will render the past acceptable."[50]

As another aspect of his Asokan identity, Premadasa portrayed himself as a Buddhist leader who was concerned about the poor, who coincidentally voted for him in large numbers. His housing schemes and garment factory schemes enabled him to portray himself in this light. To be sure, Premadasa did initiate social welfare projects that seemed to embody Buddhist values. Some of these projects arose from his prior cooperation with Sarvodaya when he served as Prime Minister. Despite these highly touted programs aimed at the poor, however, Premadasa did not actually base his economic or social policies on Buddhist principles. Perhaps even more than Jayawardene, Premadasa pursued the policies of an open-market economy. He saw no conflict in professing simultaneously the virtues of Buddhism and capitalism, because Buddhism to him was a matter of individual morality and ritual practice. Citing the example of Asoka again, Premadasa said that the great king never sought "to legislate the Dharma."[51] In the end, under Premadasa's regime, Buddhism came to be what Stanley Tambiah termed "political Buddhism," which is "Buddhism in its militant, populist, fetishized form . . . emptied of much of its normative and humane ethic."[52]

Premadasa's Campaign Against Sarvodaya

Johan Galtung pointed out that the state never likes to have rivals. He observed, "The state originally was the successor to the emperor and the emperor was the successor to God, and both God and the emperor were very jealous of all rivals."[53] This truth seems to have applied particularly well to President Premadasa, who saw his identity as the chief representative of both the religion and the state. Premadasa used the full force of the state to oppose both his enemies and his rivals. He used violent force against both the JVP and the LTTE. Premadasa also sought to nullify any domestic opposition, and for this reason he began a campaign of attacks against both Sarvodaya in general and Ariyaratne in particular.

Premadasa recognized that Ariyaratne posed a threat to his spiritual and political leadership, especially among the poor who had been a major factor in electing him. When Ariyaratne declined to assist his campaign, Premadasa's newly formed suspicions of him were undoubtedly reinforced by *The Power Pyramid and the Dharmic Cycle;* although it did not mention Premadasa by name, it sharply critiqued the government of which Premadasa was a part. Premadasa's campaign of attacks against Sarvodaya invoked his own claim to be the protector of Buddhism and charged, among other things, that Ariyaratne and his Movement were polluting the religion and endangering the Buddhist nation.

One of the most visible and forceful methods of attack used by Premadasa's government was a well-planned media campaign that directly targeted the sources of Ariyaratne's charisma and Sarvodaya's popularity, their commitment to dharmic values, and their renunciation of materialism and wealth. Representing the viewpoint of political Buddhism, the government-controlled media attempted to repudiate Ariyaratne's image as a Buddhist reformer who followed Gandhi, eschewing material wealth and regarding the spiritual truths of the Dharma as the only real wealth. Front page stories in the government newspapers portrayed Ariyaratne as a false guru who used the Dharma only to enrich himself. A particularly malicious story compared Ariyaratne to another Sri Lankan man who had fraudulently posed as a guru in England. The story said both Ariyaratne and the false guru had "used the most sacred tenets of Eastern spirituality to pile up fortunes."[54]

Another series of stories ran under a banner headline proclaiming that, "Sarvodaya Sells Lankan Children Abroad."[55] The gist of this series had been taken from an article that appeared in a West German tabloid magazine seven years earlier. Even that tabloid eventually conceded that Sarvodaya actually was innocent of these charges. Nevertheless, the government press dredged up this charge to blacken Sarvodaya's reputation. Even though Ariyaratne issued an immediate denial and rebuttal, the accusation continued to resurface in the press in various forms for the next few years. In its attempts to stigmatize Ariyaratne and Sarvodaya as "other" and as threats to the national interest, some government press stories also charged Sarvodaya with misusing development funds to supply arms to the LTTE. One paper combined some of these themes by labeling Ariyaratne the "Maharishi from Moratuwa" and saying that "spiritual leaders of the caliber of Buddha and Christ, without setting up trust funds in their names" or funneling funds to aggressors, have shown the way to change humanity.[56]

In addition to the media campaign, the government attempted to shut down the Sarvodaya Movement by limiting its freedom and its ability to function in the country. Key government ministries suddenly refused to assist Sarvodaya in any way, citing bureaucratic regulations that had not previously been a barrier. For example, the national radio and television stations ceased covering any Sarvodaya events and cancelled Ariyaratne's weekly educational radio program. The Immigration Department made it difficult for anyone connected with Sarvodaya to enter or leave the country. Other government departments, such as the Criminal Investigation Department (CID), the Labor Department, the Bribery Commission, the Environmental Authority, and the Income Tax Department, enforced new or seldom-used rules and summoned Sarvodaya officials for questioning. The

CID in particular made countless visits to Sarvodaya centers and took many people into its offices for interrogation. These questioning sessions frequently went on for hours; in the worst case, two women were detained under extremely inhumane conditions for two months. In addition, the leaders of Sarvodaya received several death threats from individuals who came to their doors wearing military or police uniforms. Tightening the screws financially, the government and the Central Bank cancelled many of Sarvodaya's loans and compelled some foreign agencies to cancel their funding of Sarvodaya's projects. When asked by Sarvodaya members to explain why they were carrying out these actions, the government officials replied that they were doing these things on "orders from above."

The capstone of the government's campaign of attacks was put in place when Premadasa appointed a Presidential Commission of Inquiry of Nongovernmental Organizations. This commission was set up, at least in theory, to investigate wrongdoing by any NGOs in the country; in actuality its primary purpose seems to have been to attack the Sarvodaya Movement and Ariyaratne and to prove they were indeed guilty of the offenses the press had charged them with. Seeing it as a way to prove their innocence, the Sarvodaya leaders at first welcomed this commission; however, they soon recognized that the commissioners were also acting "under orders from above" and would be unable to give Sarvodaya a fair hearing. Faced with this direct threat and witnessing the suffering of the country under Premadasa's regime, Ariyaratne spoke out against the government and called for "nonviolent direct action within the law and nonpartisan people's politics."

To counter the government's attack, Ariyaratne took his case directly to the people by arranging an energetic schedule of rallies and speeches in villages and towns throughout the country. It was not unusual for him to appear at five or six rallies per day, where he delivered fiery attacks on the government and set out Sarvodaya's alternative vision of social revolution. Thousands of rural supporters turned out to hear Ariyaratne charge that the government had lost its moral legitimacy to rule and had no grounds to attack the Sarvodaya Movement. Ariyaratne explained that there are three kinds of law: the law of the state, the law of the people, and the law of Dharma. Countering the government's accusations against Sarvodaya, Ariyaratne argued that the law of Dharma and the law of the people are higher than the law of the state; and when the law of the state violates the two higher forms of law, the people have a responsibility to oppose the government. On this basis, he charged that, because the President had used violence against the people and pursued economic and environmental policies that created structural violence, he had lost his dharmic mandate to serve as the leader of a Buddhist country.[57]

The Demonstration at Kandalama and Its Aftereffects

In addition to the village rallies, Sarvodaya organized peace marches, Shramadana camps, and other nonviolent demonstrations in opposition to the government. The most dramatic confrontation occurred at Kandalama, a village near the ancient Buddhist cave temple and sacred site at Dambulla. It demonstrated the way the Buddhist government attempted to cast Sarvodaya as an "other" as well as the ways that Sarvodaya fought back against the government on Buddhist grounds.

The confrontation concerned a proposal by a corporation to build a massive luxury hotel complex near Kandalama. This proposal had been approved by the government in the interest of increasing tourism. Having seen the disastrous impact that similar tourist developments had had on previously tranquil village areas, the local villagers led by the Venerable Inamaluve Sumangala, head monk of the Dambulla Buddhist temple, appealed to the government to cancel the plans for the hotel. The monk and his followers argued that such a large hotel would adversely affect the cultural and moral environment of the community; disrupt the ecological balance of the semiwilderness area where one of the last wild herds of elephants in the country lived; pollute the water supply; and infringe on the sanctity of the ancient, sacred Buddhist shrine.

Sumangala, who was also the Chair of Sarvodaya's Council of Elders, appealed to Sarvodaya to assist him in this cause. Sumangala and Ariyaratne decided to hold a *satyagraha* (peaceful demonstration) at Dambulla to protest this development project. A Catholic group led by Father Oswald Firth also joined the protest movement, because they had recently fought the government over a similar development project in a Christian area at Iranawila, on the west coast of Sri Lanka. Therefore, on July 12, 1992 thousands of Sri Lankans, Buddhists, and Christians, many of them Sarvodaya followers, assembled at the *Dambulla Rājā Mahā Vihāra* and peacefully demonstrated their opposition to the government's plans to build the tourist hotel. Buddhist monks and Catholic priests spoke against the hotel and the government, and then led the people in peaceful meditation.

The aftereffects of the satyagraha were quite interesting, with both the government and Sarvodaya jockeying to be seen as the true supporters of Buddhism. Premadasa's government, which had proclaimed itself the savior of the Dharma and the sāsana, found itself in the position of opposing Ariyaratne, Sumangala, and all of the Buddhists who protested that a sacred area would be violated by the hotel complex. Even worse, the government appeared to be opposing the Buddhists on this issue even though it had previously given in to the Catholics when they made a similar protest about a development project in their area. Sarvodaya and its allies appeared at first to have clearly put the government on the defensive. In response, Premadasa tried staging his own pro-government demonstration at Dambulla to explain how the hotel would benefit the people, but it was poorly attended and seemed clearly to be a defensive gesture.

Then someone in the government discovered a photo that had been taken at the satyagraha, showing some Catholic nuns holding aloft a large cross in front of the Dambulla Buddhist cave temple. The government used this picture to regain the high ground as the defender of Buddhism. Posters displaying this photo suddenly appeared, plastered on billboards and walls all over the country. The posters also had this statement, "Sarvodaya profiteering businessman *(mudalali)* Ariyaratne and the rogue monk *(hora sangeya)* Sumangala took the cross to Dambulla."

The government papers also ran the picture, along with editorials denouncing the action that it showed as an affront to Buddhism and proclaiming that "the organisers had desecrated a Buddhist sacred area and polluted a Buddhist environment by allowing other religionists to display a cross in the precincts of the Dambulla Rājā Mahā Vihāra."[58] Other stories charged that Sarvodaya, Sumangala, and the other leaders had attempted to create ethnic strife by displaying Christian symbols in a Buddhist temple. The papers cited monks who voiced the government's argument. One head monk asked, "Will the Buddhist clergy ever be allowed to display the Buddhist flag and perform satyagraha in the Vatican?" Another head monk from Anuradhapura declared that the president "who created a separate Ministry for Buddha Sāsana is doing a great service for the country. It is wrong to conduct such agitations when the President is making a genuine effort to develop all places of religious worship."[59] The government stories did not bother to explain that the Christians had received permission from the Buddhist leaders to carry the cross in the procession, and they did not cite the many monks and leaders of the Sangha who approved of the satyagraha.

❀ ❀ ❀

In the end, as with many political events, the meaning and significance of the Kandalama demonstration remains open to interpretation. H. L. Seneviratne explained it as a kind of social drama engineered by Sumangala to capture public support for his attempt to create a new chapter of the Sangha to be based in the Dambulla temple. "Stated differently, the protest was a rite of passage . . . that ordained the Dambulla chapter to full and autonomous cultural and political adulthood."[60] Sumangala had been attempting to liberate the Dambulla temple from the hegemony of the Asgiriya branch of the Siyam Nikaya.[61] He proclaimed the Dambulla temple to be the chief temple of a new chapter of the Siyam Nikaya called *Rangiri Dambulu Sangha Sabhava* (The Sangha Assembly of the Golden Rock of Dambulla").[62] Seneviratne argued that, although Sumangala and his Dambulla monks had already declared their independence from the Asgiriya temple and gone to court to assert and defend their autonomy, they needed to gain public acceptance of their new status. The hotel debate served to cast Sumangala in the role of a "David taking on the Goliath of big business and no less a power than the government."[63] The themes of the protest—"agro-economy, culture, and environment"—were perfectly suited to enabling Sumangala and his supporters to capture the support of the urban middle class and the local villagers. Seneviratne summarized his interpretation of the satyagraha, saying:

> "This was no longer a protest against the establishment of a tourist hotel beside a scenic man-made lake in the vicinity of a monastery, which is an ancient Buddhist site. It never was. In fact what we see is a brilliant and resourceful monk, trying to gain legitimacy for his newly established subsect by attracting the attention of elite members of the society."[64]

If one accepts Seneviratne's interpretation of Sumangala's motives, then one must ask how they affected Ariyaratne's role in this social drama. Was Sumangala simply using Ariyaratne and his Sarvodaya supporters to further the goals of the Dambulla monks? Was Ariyaratne using Sumangala for his own purposes? It seems probable that both Sumangala and Ariyaratne saw the hotel debate as a golden opportunity to gain public support for their own causes. Since Ariyaratne was, at the time, already in the villages defending himself against the government's attacks, Kandalama provided him with an even larger stage on which to perform a social drama that would highlight his opposition to the Premadasa government. Although

Seneviratne casts doubt on Sumangala's sincerity in advocating the environmental, cultural, and economic issues surrounding Kandalama, there can be no doubt about Ariyaratne's sincerity on these points. If Kandalama provided a good opportunity for Ariyaratne to take his case to the public, it also provided an opportunity for him to speak out on some of the key issues that Sarvodaya stood for: village culture, environmentalism, and opposition to the top-down economic policies of the government.

Sarvodaya Launches Its Alternative Political System

The clash with the government brought into focus the contrast between Premadasa's nationalistic Buddhism and the socially engaged Buddhism of Sarvodaya. The government accused Ariyaratne of vitiating his claim to be a religious leader by becoming involved in political issues, such as the debate over the tourist hotel or the government's conduct of the war. Ariyaratne replied, "What the government considers politics, I consider the welfare of the people and the protection of the Dhamma."[65] Labeling the government's charges and attacks on the Movement *adharmic*, Ariyaratne renewed his call for a nonviolent revolution that would establish the law of the people.

At the Annual General Meeting of the Sarvodaya Movement in December 1992, Ariyaratne declared that he was "launching a new political process through Sarvodaya" that would create a different political order in the country.[66] They would mobilize Sarvodaya to generate a "critical mass of spiritual consciousness" to build a participatory democracy. He argued that the current system of "power and party politics" had become destructive and was incompatible with Sri Lankan culture. In a guest editorial in the newspaper, Ariyaratne stated his reasons for seeking to implement an alternative system. He wrote, "If we only consider the fear psychosis that prevails in this country from the lowest to the highest and the blood that has freely flowed during the past decade, that itself is enough for us to realize that the time is ripe for a heart-searching and a reconstruction of our polity and its twin brother the economy."[67] Saying that Sarvodaya must not fear "to embark on a new political path and should even resort to direct nonviolent action if necessary," Ariyaratne sent the youth corps of the Movement out to promote Sarvodaya's alternative political order.[68]

Ariyaratne's vision of a new polity invoked the Gandhian ideal of an "ocean of self-sufficient villages" or "a commonwealth of village republics" that would be linked together in a loose confederation that constitutes a participatory democracy.[69] One of the major requirements of this kind of participatory democracy, Ariyaratne claimed, is the abolition of the current system of party politics. In his writings and speeches he has proposed to change the system: "Sarvodaya rejects the existing system of party politics . . . Sarvodaya will strive to build from the village upwards an alternative people's participatory and democratic political structure."[70]

Ariyaratne believes that the system of party politics represents a legacy from the colonial rulers that has become a vehicle for the elite to maintain their power over the rural people. He wrote, "The system of party politics that has been organised in this country . . . has done enormous damage to our people over the last forty years."[71] To replace the party politics system, Ariyaratne proposed a system of consensus politics, the model for which he also borrowed from Gandhi and Vinoba Bhave. Ariyaratne described this as "Gandhiji's brilliant concept of village self-government."[72] He wrote, Sarvodaya seeks a "political system of consensus from the village level right up to the level of national political decision making. It is a system of evolution of power from the bottom up."[73]

Consensus politics differs from party politics in that it embodies local values, unites the people rather than divides them, and leads to peace rather than conflict. It is a truly decentralized system, not imposed from above with propaganda and coercion, but arising from the people. Whereas the party political system views the village communities as peripheral to the political process, Sarvodaya's consensus system views them as central. Ariyaratne sees this kind of political system arising when the Movement develops "a sufficiently large number of such [Sarvodaya] communities in all parts of the country that are powerful enough to influence national policy." Ariyaratne hopes that the Sri Lankan Sarvodaya Movement can facilitate a network of twenty-five thousand independent village republics to generate bottom-up power to challenge the top-down power of the government and the multinational corporations.[74] When this kind of consensus political system develops in the village, the village network will have the potential for national and global governance.

With Ariyaratne stumping the rural areas calling for political change, the Sri Lankan press began to speculate about his potential role in a consensus political system. One newspaper reported the results of an earlier political survey showing that Ariyaratne's popularity as a political figure ranked second only to that of Jayawardene, who was president at the time.[75] Another newspaper story declared that Ariyaratne "had already hinted that he was willing to be the consensus candidate in case of a tussle between the various opposition parties on the selection of a candidate."[76] Ariyaratne does seem to have dropped hints about his availability to serve in a new political system. In *The Power Pyramid and the Dharmic Cycle,* he wrote that the leadership for the new consensus system of politics would come from "a set of self-sacrificing, intelligent people . . . who have accepted local value systems and who respect the sovereignty of the people."[77]

Even after the death of Premadasa in 1993, the rumors about Ariyaratne's candidacy continued. In his reply to a letter from Sarvodaya's foreign donors asking him to clarify whether he intended to run for the presidency, Ariyaratne said he had no intention of running for the office; he only sought to empower the poor. At a speaking engagement a few years later, when an audience member asked if he would accept a nomination for president, Ariyaratne replied that he would, only if they were able to change the political system and the people invited him to serve. He added, however, that he would prefer to be more like Gandhi and guide the new leaders who would emerge.[78] At that time, Ariyaratne seemed to opt for what Sallie King called "the prophetic voice" as a way of trying to influence the political process and bring about a new political system in Sri Lanka.[79]

Millennialist Predictions about the Political System

In addition to calling for a new political system, Ariyaratne predicted that the current social, political, and economic systems of the country will collapse in the near future. He made this prediction as early as 1988 in *The Power Pyramid and the Dharmic Cycle.* In this book, he employed a series of diagrams to trace what he regarded as the degeneration of the power pyramid in Sri Lanka, from independence in the 1940s to the contemporary period (see Figures 4.1 and 4.2). In the early period, this pyramid was balanced with the leadership at the apex, resting firmly on a base of popular support; but in the current situation the leadership at the top has both expanded and lost almost all contact with the people at the base.[80] Describing this situation, Ariyaratne declared that, "Sarvodaya sees the prevailing social order in Sri Lanka as resembling a steep power pyramid with a very narrow base of people's participation that makes the power structure unstable and liable to crash."[81]

In various articles and speeches during the 1990s, Ariyaratne repeated this apocalyptic vision about the impending failure of the existing structures. For example, in a July 1994 speech to the Central Bank in Colombo, he predicted that both the political system and the entire

4.1   The Power Pyramid that arose after Independence in 1948.

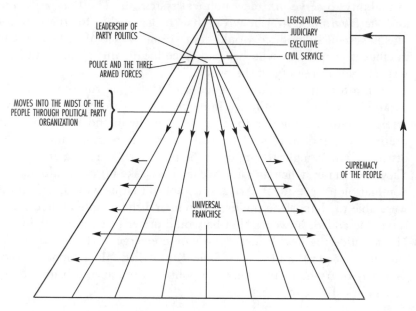

From. A. T. Ariyaratne, *The Power Pyramid and the Dharmic Cycle* (Ratmalana: Sarvodaya Vishva Lekha Press, 1988), 120.

economic system would break down before the year 2000. When that happens, he said, Sarvodaya will have already prepared the villages of the country to survive with a new system of people's participatory democracy.[82] In a 1997 speech in Colombo, he expanded the scope and lengthened the time frame, predicting that the political system and the world economy would crash in at least ten years because of the increasing complexity of the systems and the lack of people's participation. The corollary to the destruction of the present order, in Ariyaratne's view, is that a new order, a dharmic Sarvodaya social order, would emerge from the ruins.[83]

In these prophecies, Ariyaratne has taken a Gandhian theme (the power pyramid) and combined it with a form of postcolonial millennialism. Charles Keyes noted three classic characteristics of millennialism: a prediction of the imminent and "radical destruction of the existing social order," the promise of a new order, and the coming of a savior figure.[84] Seeking to explain the causes for historical millennial movements, Keyes suggested that "millennial movements emerge during a

4.2   The Change in the Power Pyramid: 1970–88.

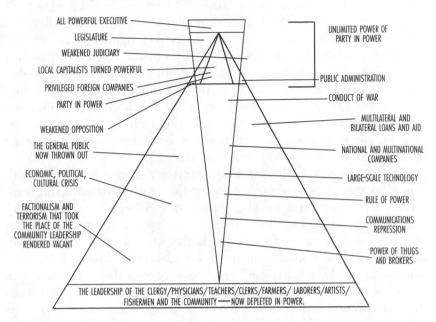

From. A. T. Ariyaratne, *The Power Pyramid and the Dharmic Cycle*
(Ratmalana: Sarvodaya Vishva Lekha Press, 1988), 122.

crisis centering around conceptions of power."[85] He goes on to say that
"for Burma and Ceylon, the colonial experience—which saw the elimination of the Buddhist monarchy—has provided the crucible within
which millennial dispositions have been forged."[86] Ariyaratne's prophecies of an apocalyptic crash follow the pattern outlined by Keyes: They
are based on a perception of "a crisis centering around a conception of
power" in Sri Lanka that began with the colonial experience and continued as postcolonial governments perpetuated colonial and capitalist
policies.

Ariyaratne clearly expresses the first two of Keyes' characteristics of
millennialism, but he is somewhat vague about the third, the savior
figure. Since Ariyaratne's prophecies do not mention Metteyya (the
Buddha to be born) explicitly, they do not represent "traditional
Buddhist millennialism" in the sense that Steven Collins described it.
Collins pointed out that traditional (Theravada) Buddhist millennialism
involves necessarily "Buddhist ideas of future felicity associated with
Metteyya and other future Buddhas."[87] Although they lack such references

to the future Buddha, Ariyaratne's prophecies have clear links to varieties of Sinhala Buddhist millennialism.[88] In Sri Lanka, during the Buddhist resurgence of the 1950s, for example, beliefs about a predestined renewal of the Dharma and the appearance of a righteous ruler (Prince Diyasena) featured prominently in the Sinhala Buddhist ideology that Sarvodaya inherited and retains to some extent.[89] Such millennial predictions could be seen to represent Sarvodaya's longing for the restoration of what Anne Hansen described as an "idealized conception of meaning and order."[90] However, rather than resorting to force to bring this restoration about, as many millennial movements have, Sarvodaya turned to Gandhian ideals of a nonviolent revolution.

For the Sarvodaya Movement, Ariyaratne's prophecies have significance, because they legitimize the quest for a village-based social revolution. When the crash occurs, Sarvodaya's vision of a self-sufficient participatory democracy located in the villages will be seen, not as utopian, but pragmatic and realistic. In the Strategic Plan for 1995–98, Ariyaratne noted that the open market economy which "thrives on competition and individualism" produces a current that runs counter to Sarvodaya's aim of creating a no-affluence, no-poverty society. But when the crash occurs, that current will be reversed. Ariyaratne wrote that, as "the political and economic superstructure continues to disintegrate, the relatively autonomous community structures will be able to meet the basic and secondary needs of the people . . . [W]e will seek to tread this path to a new society by the year 2001."[91]

Ariyaratne's millennial vision provides a context that links Sarvodaya's peace movement and its call for a nonviolent people's revolution. Clearly it is with this vision in mind that Sarvodaya launched its village revolution focusing on "10,000 villages" and has implemented programs to bring financial independence and stability to villages, while ushering in a new social order. It is also in this context that Sarvodaya issued its call for a consensus political system that will bring about a change of leadership in the country.

CHAPTER FIVE

THE ROAD AHEAD:
DESHODAYA, NATIONAL AWAKENING

Having surveyed the road that Sarvodaya has followed in developing its vision to this point, we can now ask where does the road lead from here? How is Sarvodaya interpreting its vision and shaping its program in the present context of the new millennium? What does Sarvodaya's vision have to offer to Sri Lanka and the world, both now and in the future? How viable is Sarvodaya's vision in a contemporary context that is dominated by globalization, an open market economy, and an unresolved ethnic conflict? What challenges do these forces present for Sarvodaya's vision at present and in the future, and how is Sarvodaya changing to meet these challenges?

Over two decades after Denis Goulet wrote about "Sarvodaya at the Crossroads," Sarvodaya can be said to stand again at a new crossroads because of the many changes taking place in the nation and in the Movement itself.[1] While still trying to resolve the long ethnic conflict and achieve peace, Sri Lanka is simultaneously contending with the forces of globalization and open market economics; although they are also sweeping the rest of the world, they are creating especially acute economic and political problems for Sri Lankans. From Sarvodaya's perspective, most of the effects of these global economic and political forces run counter to Sarvodaya's vision for society. In its Comprehensive Plan for 2000–05, Sarvodaya notes that the Movement is still very much focused on achieving its vision of "a no-poverty, no-affluence society based on the Gandhian values of truth, nonviolence, and self sacrifice."[2] Sarvodaya's leaders recognize, however, that globalization and its allied forces are creating a society in which the gap between poverty and affluence is widening daily and where the dominant values increasingly represent the opposites of truth, nonviolence, and self-sacrifice.

In the present context, however, Sarvodaya has become a huge NGO reaching—according to its own figures—almost fifteen thousand villages in the country, and its leaders now believe that it has built up sufficient critical mass to mount some opposition to the effects of globalization, Westernization, consumerism, and other transnational forces.[3] Sarvodaya's leaders feel that it should be able to use its voice to advance its own vision, instead of just passively accepting the vision of global economics as translated and implemented by the government and the multinational forces.

When Goulet wrote in the early 1980s, he saw Sarvodaya standing at a crossroads that called for the Movement to choose whether to retain Sarvodaya's integrity by working on its own terms in the villages or attain a national scope by cooperating with the government on development programs. The choices Sarvodaya confronts at this new crossroads differ from the earlier ones. They represent the options of either continuing to work in the villages to offset or counteract the effects of the present system or trying to transform the present system that the government and international forces have created. In actuality, however, these two options are not competing, because Sarvodaya has decided that it must try to do both. While not abandoning its village development and relief projects, Sarvodaya has determined that it must go forward and try to realize its vision on the national and international levels. It hopes to transcend the government and the global forces that it believes are leading society in the wrong direction. Sarvodaya's leaders recognize that there are many NGOs in the country that can carry out development projects on the village level, but they feel that Sarvodaya may be the only NGO with sufficient strength and vision to chart a new direction for society.

A. T. Ariyaratne explains the rationale for this plan: As Buddhists living in Sri Lanka, with its long Buddhist heritage, they must do what engaged Buddhists are doing all over the world; apply Buddhist ideals to solve concrete, contemporary problems. He says,

> "We have to awaken ourselves to a Buddhist Vision for the Future without losing any more time, and execute our responsibilities to our people and to the world by taking initiatives to change and transform society. We cannot leave it to chance or fate. We cannot leave it in the hands of governments, political parties, generals, bureaucrats, technocrats, businessmen or even teachers, parents, professionals and the priesthood. This initiative has to be taken by men and women as individuals who have a vision of planetary consciousness and interrelationship with everything in nature."[4]

The vision is not new for Sarvodaya; what is new is Sarvodaya's conviction that now there is a genuine possibility of actualizing it. With the strength it has built up, Sarvodaya feels it must seek deshodaya and *vishvodaya* (world awakening). After more than forty years of following the vision and building up the Movement, Sarvodaya believes the time is right to try to implement the vision for the good of all by empowering the people at the grassroots.

To implement this vision, Sarvodaya has identified three elements or areas that must be addressed: consciousness, economics, and power. Sarvodaya highlighted these three elements in its Peace Action Plan published in 2001, noting that they represent not only the elements that lead to peace, but also the elements that constitute and determine the nature of any society.[5] If these three elements are positive and in balance, a society will be good; if they are negative and out of balance, a society will be negative (See Figure 5.1).

Sarvodaya diagnoses the current problems in Sri Lankan society, including the war and the related factors such as poverty and violence, as manifestations of "a lack of holistic social health" stemming from an imbalance in these three elements.[6] In order to achieve peace and positive holistic social health, these three elements must be addressed and brought into balance. Sarvodaya's current plans and programs emphasize what they must do in each of these areas to realize the vision and bring about a civil society that expresses a Sarvodaya social order.

Consciousness

From the outset, Sarvodaya began with consciousness as the key to the awakening of individuals and society. Sarvodaya retains this emphasis on spirituality in its present attempt to implement a new social order. Consciousness represents the starting point in Sarvodaya's plan to transform society by building up a civil society in the villages. Sarvodaya seeks to instill a new spiritual vision to provide the foundation for a spiritual infrastructure that will establish holistic social health. In Ariyaratne's view, transforming the consciousness of individuals and communities toward compassion and peace represents an essential step toward building a just and peaceful world.[7] In a key speech in 2002, entitled "A Buddhist Vision for the Future," Ariyaratne equated the essence of a Buddhist vision with this notion of a positive state of consciousness. He said. "What I mean by a vision is a state of dynamic consciousness directed towards achieving peace and happiness for one and all. This is a '*Dassana*' (an insight) and not a '*diṭṭhi*' (an ideology)."[8]

Sarvodaya's approach to generating a critical mass of spiritual consciousness has focused on the peace meditations and the new peace

5.1   War and violence are fueled by the interplay of these three factors:

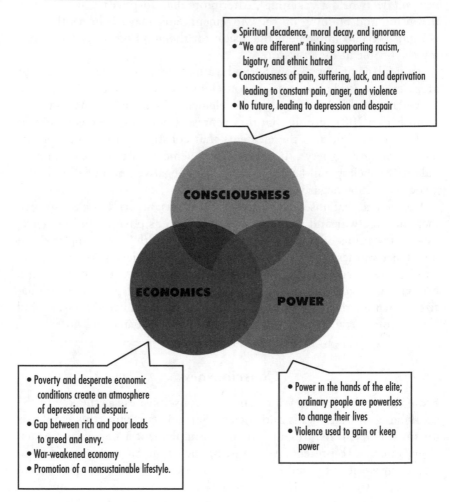

- Spiritual decadence, moral decay, and ignorance
- "We are different" thinking supporting racism, bigotry, and ethnic hatred
- Consciousness of pain, suffering, lack, and deprivation leading to constant pain, anger, and violence
- No future, leading to depression and despair

CONSCIOUSNESS

ECONOMICS

POWER

- Poverty and desperate economic conditions create an atmosphere of depression and despair.
- Gap between rich and poor leads to greed and envy.
- War-weakened economy
- Promotion of a nonsustainable lifestyle.

- Power in the hands of the elite; ordinary people are powerless to change their lives
- Violence used to gain or keep power

From Dr. Vinya Ariyaratne, *The Sarvodaya Peace Action Plan*, (Ratmalana, Sri Lanka: Sarvodaya Vishva Lekha Press, n. d.), 9.

center, Vishva Niketan. Vishva Niketan serves as an anchor for the Movement to remind it of the importance of spirituality and to summon the people to meditate. But it has been the large peace meditations that have served as the primary means for generating and demonstrating this spiritual consciousness. These mass gatherings for peace demonstrate the breadth and depth of Sarvodaya's spiritual vision and the potential the Movement has for effecting change in the structures of power.

Although Sarvodaya affirms the spiritual power of the peace meditations for changing people's consciousness, it also recognizes their political influence. Sarvodaya has specifically said that to influence the national discussion, "Sarvodaya's power must be visible in a way that the political parties—and the people—understand."[9] The government media has taken note of Sarvodaya's power in these meditations, viewing it at times favorably and at other times critically. The *Daily News,* for example, observed that the peace meditations represent "a further sign that civil society is alerting itself to the need for peace."[10] But another paper criticized the meditations as futile and described Ariyaratne as "one of the last Gandhians on Earth."[11] That the power and potential of Sarvodaya's campaign has been noticed by the political and religious establishments in Sri Lanka, however, was clearly shown by the events that surrounded Sarvodaya's 2002 peace meditation in Kandy.

The Kandy Peace Meditation

In summer 2002, Sarvodaya began to make plans to hold a peace meditation in front of the Daḷadā Māligāva, the Temple of the Tooth in Kandy. The meditation was scheduled for August 22. It was to be the next large meditation gathering after the massive peace meditation in Anuradhapura the previous March. In preparation for the Kandy meditation, Sarvodaya obtained permission for the gathering from the *Diyavadana Nilamē*, the lay administrator of the temple, and from one of the monastic leaders, the *Mahanayaka* of the Asgiriya Nikāya.

Sarvodaya's plans became controversial when someone sent an anonymous letter to the temple, charging that Sarvodaya was planning to bring LTTE (Liberation Tigers of Tamil Eelam) supporters there to meditate. Soon posters began to appear on buildings and walls in Kandy calling on Buddhists to protect the Temple of the Tooth from "pseudo-meditation campaigners." When these objections arose, the Nilamē withdrew his permission for Sarvodaya to assemble in front of the temple and issued orders for the police to prevent Sarvodaya from bringing banners or loudspeakers into the area. As the day approached, however, Sarvodaya and the Nilamē reached a compromise that allowed Sarvodaya to hold its meditation in another area adjacent to the temple.

When Sarvodaya's supporters went to Kandy on August 22, some of them were turned back by police and protesters before they reached the temple area, but about a thousand people assembled near the temple to hold the peace meditation. As they began to meditate, however, a group of young lay persons and young monks began to verbally assault the meditators in an attempt to disrupt the assembly. It was a striking scene: The Sarvodaya members wore white and sat quietly on the ground, while the young men led by several young monks—the protectors of Buddhism—confronted them with verbal insults and threats. The attackers, who seemed to come from a variety of right-wing Sinhala Buddhist and nationalist groups, questioned the Buddhist credentials of the Sarvodaya meditators and challenged their right to meditate at the temple. Believing that any support for the peace process amounts to support for the LTTE, the right-wing protesters charged that the Sarvodayans were not true Buddhists and were aiding the LTTE by this assembly. The protesters also attacked the meditators for bringing Christians, Hindus, and Muslims to the temple to meditate.

After about an hour, the police had to break up the assembly, because the protesters were becoming more hostile, crowding around the seated Sarvodaya meditators, and threatening them. The police finally escorted the Sarvodaya members to safety as the protesters jeered. Undaunted by the experience, however, Ariyaratne had the last word, telling the reporters on the scene that it had been the most successful peace meditation yet. The Kandy meditation demonstrated again that Sarvodaya comprises a critical mass of individuals who have a spiritual consciousness and are willing to take risks for peace and for their vision of the way society should be ordered. It was not the largest demonstration that Sarvodaya has held, but it made its point and received considerable attention in the national media and press. The meditation undoubtedly demonstrated to the government and the right wing Buddhists that Sarvodaya does possess spiritual force. The opposition to the meditation reflected the recognition by the Sangha and the politicians that Sarvodaya's assemblies have the power to shape public opinion.

Sarvodaya's Spirituality and Religious Pluralism

Although the protesters who confronted Sarvodaya in Kandy were largely politically motivated, some of the questions they raised are significant for our understanding of Sarvodaya's mission and identity today. For example, although we should not take the protesters' challenge of Sarvodaya's Buddhist credentials too seriously, the underlying question is one that Sarvodaya itself wrestles with at present: Is

Sarvodaya today a Buddhist movement or is it an ecumenical movement? A. T. Ariyaratne has maintained that Sarvodaya's spiritual vision and spiritual consciousness are not exclusively Buddhist, but ecumenical. In his writings he has made it clear that the Sarvodaya Movement is not restricted to Sinhalese Buddhists, because "Sarvodaya is the essence of all religions and therefore the adherents of various religions and people belonging to various ethnic communities engage in its services as members of one family."[12] He also says that people of various faiths are all claimants to the common culture that he has been describing. Dr. Vinya Ariyaratne, as the new Executive Director of Sarvodaya, has shown an interest in both retaining the spiritual character of the Movement and working to make Sarvodaya more inclusive of other religions. In its Comprehensive Plan for 2000–05, Sarvodaya expressed the view that "much of Sri Lanka is Buddhist, however, the Sarvodaya principles are completely compatible with Hinduism and, we believe, with the teachings of Christianity, Islam, Baha'i, and all other major faiths."[13]

Although Sarvodaya's leaders proclaim it to be an ecumenical rather than a Buddhist movement and the protesters in Kandy regarded it, for different reasons, in somewhat the same way, one can still ask to what extent Sarvodaya's vision is genuinely inclusive. Does it accept the views of the other religions or does it merely subsume them under a kind of Buddhist-Victorian spiritualism? To gain more perspective on this matter one can ask how other religious groups in Sri Lanka regard Sarvodaya. Do they see it as a Buddhist movement? How do the members of other religions view Sarvodaya's peace meditations, and its attempts to build a spiritual consciousness as the basis for a new social order? What is the role of other religions in Sarvodaya's vision of a dharmic society? To explore these questions, I interviewed members of other, non-Buddhist religions in Sri Lanka, both inside and outside the Sarvodaya Movement. Their answers provide another perspective on Sarvodaya's current identity and its quest to build a dharmic society that includes all groups.[14] What follows is a summary of the interviews.

Non-Buddhists who are employed by Sarvodaya almost unanimously said that Sarvodaya is not a Buddhist organization. They feel it is ecumenical and open to all religions. However, many of them qualified their statements, saying that before they began working with Sarvodaya they did think it was Buddhist. Before he joined Sarvodaya, one Muslim thought it was Buddhist because of its peace meditations and philosophy. Other Muslims are often surprised when he tells them he works with Sarvodaya because they regard it as Buddhist. Another Muslim said

Sarvodaya may have been Buddhist when it began, but now it works with all groups. A Hindu in the organization also said Sarvodaya is not a Buddhist organization, but embraces all religions and is especially compatible with Hinduism.

Non-Buddhists outside of the Sarvodaya Movement were almost equally unanimous in their view that Sarvodaya is a Buddhist organization. A Tamil Hindu from the north said Tamils tend to regard Sarvodaya as a form of Sinhala Buddhism because of its philosophy and its history. He pointed to a Hindu group in Jaffna that split off from Sarvodaya and formed a Hindu-based movement called North Lanka Sarvodaya. Muslims outside the Movement agreed that Sarvodaya is perceived in the Muslim community as a Sinhala Buddhist organization. To them, this means that Sarvodaya has to work to gain the trust of Muslims.

Most Christians also view Sarvodaya as a Buddhist organization. A Methodist pastor said people in the north and east are suspicious about Sarvodaya's motives, because they regard it as another form of Sinhala Buddhism. A Catholic leader said most Catholics see Sarvodaya as a Buddhist intrusion into their areas. One Methodist leader, however, said that Sarvodaya may have begun as a Buddhist movement, but now has a wider scope and works with all groups. Father Oswald Firth, another Catholic leader, made a useful distinction; he observed that Sarvodaya may be based on Buddhist tenets, but is not an institution of Buddhism.

Given these views of Sarvodaya's identity, how do the members of the other religions regard Sarvodaya's peace meditations and its quest to build up a spiritual consciousness? Sarvodaya has included members of the other religions in all of the major peace meditations and has accorded the leaders of the other religions a prominent place at the front of these assemblies. The leaders I interviewed, who had participated in the meditations, tend to regard them very favorably. Father Firth, for example, said the peace meditations definitely moved the peace process forward. He brought one hundred priests to the first one, and since then he has participated in almost all of them. He praised them for being nonviolent assemblies of diverse people; they represent one of the most dramatic expressions of civil society in contemporary Sri Lanka. He thinks Sarvodaya should continue them now, especially because true peace has not yet arrived. Sarvodaya should redouble its efforts and take the lead in campaigning for true peace in all senses.

Some of the Muslims who participated in the meditations also view them in a positive light. There was no problem with Muslims taking part in these meditations because, "Islam has meditation also." One woman said that, when she participated, she did not feel she was either Muslim or Buddhist; she just felt a pure spirituality. The Muslims said the meditations were useful in promoting peace in the country, and served to unify the various groups that took part. Interestingly, however, they also argued that the meditations would be more effective if there were more discussion and explanation, and less silent sitting. Drawing on what seems to be an Islamic model, they said that in addition to the meditation there should be a lecture or sermon explaining the need for peace and unity.

A Methodist leader said he has no doubt that Sarvodaya's peace meditations—especially the major one in Anuradhapura—had an impact on the peace process. Other religious leaders, however, do not share these favorable views. A Hindu leader labeled them "a big show, a publicity campaign." A Christian theologian expressed a similar opinion, saying that Sarvodaya's peace meditations were just riding the wave that was created by others who had been working with the people to bring justice. Another Christian said the peace meditations had little impact on the peace process, because that process has more to do with the will of the government, the LTTE, and the foreign powers than with the actions of an NGO like Sarvodaya.

Although they participated in the peace meditations and generally support Sarvodaya's programs, the members of these other religions were not as optimistic about Sarvodaya's aim of building a spiritual consciousness that would include all religions. One exception was a Hindu informant, who said there clearly could be a common spiritual ground to the religions. As proof for his assertion, he cited Sai Baba and his approach to religious unity. Most interview participants, however, seemed to think that Sarvodaya should not assume that the peace meditations will lead to a spiritual consensus among the religions. Christians doubt that Sarvodaya can find a spiritual or theological common denominator that will be accepted by the whole church. A number of Christians said that interfaith dialogue and consensus will more likely result from working together to address social problems. The Muslim participants similarly agreed that interreligious unity could be reached more certainly by working together on practical problems. They suggested that Sarvodaya join with the Muslims and start a campaign to combat social problems, such as alcohol, gambling, environmental issues, and consumerist foreign values.

Related to this question of spiritual consensus and common ground is the question of the new social order that Sarvodaya seeks to build. Ariyaratne has employed the term Dharmadīpa to refer to this ideal social order that he hopes to bring about when Sarvodaya restores holistic health to society. Since the term derives from the Sinhala Buddhist heritage, how acceptable is it to the followers of other religions as a goal for a new social order? Most of the interview participants felt the term is too fraught with Buddhist meaning to be acceptable. Several Christian participants said that Dharmadīpa is a Buddhist term pertaining to the Buddha's prophecies for the island, and it is not acceptable to try to equate it with the Kingdom of God. Some Muslim participants expressed a similar sentiment, saying that Muslims regard Dharmadīpa as a Buddhist goal. If Sarvodaya wants to reinterpret this term to make it more universal, the burden is on Sarvodaya to explain to these other religions how this ideal can also include non-Buddhists. The Muslims viewed this term as an example of the kind of "communication gap" that has plagued Sarvodaya's relations with the Muslim community.

Some people, however, found that Sarvodaya's idea of Dharmadīpa presents no problems for their community. A Hindu, for example, said that Dharmadīpa represents an ideal that is common to all religions: an idea of heaven. A Catholic leader agreed that Dharmadīpa represents a good concept for Sarvodaya's social ideal; the term comes from the dominant Sinhala Buddhist culture, yet describes an order that would provide a place for all people.

Although Sarvodaya's peace meditations have certainly demonstrated that many people support its goal of peace, the comments of these non-Buddhists reveal a lack of clarity about whether the meditations can be regarded as manifestations of a consensus of spiritual consciousness. Many of these people interpret this spirituality in a theological sense, agreeing with Ariyaratne and his Sarvodaya colleagues' view that it forms the common denominator for all of the religions. But this sense of theological unity as the meaning of spirituality is difficult for others to endorse.

There is another sense of spirituality and spiritual consciousness, however, that may be both closer to the intentions of Sarvodaya and easier for the other religions to accept. This understanding of spirituality derives more from Gandhi, who said that "religion was secularizable through a perception of religion as spirituality."[15] Sarvodaya's Peace Action Plan seems to offer a definition of this kind of secularized spiritual consciousness that constitutes a pragmatic and moral force. Sarvodaya describes the field of consciousness as concerned with overcoming "spiritual decadence, moral decay and ignorance," as well as racism, bigotry, and ethnic hatred; while on the positive side, it has to do with "spiritual awakening, moral development, inner peace, inclusivity, and a multi-cultural outlook."[16]

Ariyaratne also described this spiritual consciousness as having to do with the interconnectedness of all life. He wrote, "Peace and happiness for one and all is dependent on all of us recognizing and accepting that we are closely linked together: A Buddhist vision of compassion and interconnectedness." Further, Ariyaratne described this state of mind by saying, "We believe that what has happened [in Sri Lanka] has been primarily due to a lack of *Mettā*."[17]

This kind of consciousness of unity and interconnectedness that leads to a moral sense of the need to address social problems seems consistent with the concerns of the non-Buddhist participants. Although they may not be willing at this point to endorse Sarvodaya's belief that there is a common spiritual unity to all religions, they nevertheless do seem to value these kinds of social and ethical outcomes of the spiritual consciousness that Sarvodaya discusses. It may be that Sarvodaya needs to work with these groups to develop interfaith dialogue and to engage in other concrete social service projects, but the foundation for what Sarvodaya understands as a critical mass of spiritual consciousness seems to be present already. All of these religions share a spiritual common denominator in their opposition to materialism, consumerism, and the oppression of people. They emphasize the importance of "being" rather than "having," and understand the need to help the poor, the downtrodden, and the oppressed.

The Buddhist concepts of mettā, karuṇā and other ideals have clear parallels in these other religions. For example, the selflessness of Buddhism (anattā) is paralleled by the Christian concept of self-emptying (kenosis). As one Christian argued, spirituality is one of the "essential languages" that can be used to unite the people to build a better world. "From a Christian perspective, I would say that the liberative core of our religions—the Dharma—is the really real that can spell the good of all, very specifically the good of the poor, the oppressed, the marginalised in all departments of human life."[18] The peace meditations have highlighted this kind of practical and ethical spiritual consciousness, and Sarvodaya can work with the various religious groups to establish a new social order that will be based on these spiritual values.

Economic and Social Empowerment

Cultivating this critical mass of spiritual consciousness, which manifests as a pragmatic, secularized spiritual consciousness, Sarvodaya seeks to develop the other two elements that it regards as essential for holistic social health: economics and power. The two terms that Sarvodaya has employed in its recent plans and programs to signify the creation of a new social order based on these elements are gram swaraj and deshodaya. In Sarvodaya's usage, the terms are closely related: gram swaraj signifies the liberation of the village through the creation of economic and social programs at the grassroots level; and deshodaya signifies the national and political outcome of this village liberation process.

In effect, Sarvodaya proposes to empower the people at the grassroots to construct a civil society that will bring a new social order embodying Gandhian and Buddhist ideals. Sarvodaya's conception of a civil society agrees to some extent with the definition suggested by Michael Walzer: "The words 'civil society' name the space of uncoerced human association and also the set of relational networks—formed for the sake of family, faith, interest, and ideology—that fill this space."[19]

Sarvodaya's idea here also resembles the conception of civil society proposed by Gordon White, that "civil society represents an intermediate associational realm between the family and the state populated by organisations which are separate from the state, enjoy autonomy in relation to the state and are formed voluntarily by members of society to protect or extend their interests and values."[20] Neither of these definitions, however, fully captures the distinctive conception of civil society that Sarvodaya has developed. Sarvodaya seeks to empower not just any civil society that will stand over against the state and the market; it seeks to create a citizenry that will embody Gandhian and Buddhist "interests and values" in generating alternatives to the state and the market. Sarvodaya wants a dharmic citizenry that will generate a cultural-spiritual revolution to build up a dharmic civil society.

Sarvodaya's discussion of gram swaraj and deshodaya follows the dual aspects of Gandhi's discourse concerning civil society: "First, his call for the secularisation of religion as a basis for civil society; and second, his view of civil society as a framework for mediating modernisation, where notions such as 'autonomy' and 'progress' are open to critique and examination."[21]

Sarvodaya has, from the outset, adhered to a Gandhian model that sought to empower the people in the villages to cope with the effects of the centralization and modernization policies promoted by the government. Sarvodaya's leaders have argued that the colonial powers destroyed the traditional horizontal axis of village power in order to build up a vertical axis of governmental hierarchy, a pattern that postcolonial governments have continued. From Sarvodaya's perspective, the recent waves of globalization and modernization have further reinforced the hierarchical structures by imposing a layer of economic and consumerist oppression on top of the subjugation of the people by the government hierarchy. Thus, the people at the grass roots are trapped between oppressive state forces and oppressive market forces.

Sarvodaya seeks to empower the people at the grass roots to liberate themselves from the control of both the state and the market. Sarvodaya wants to show the people how to build—or, in Sarvodaya's view, rebuild—a dharmic civil society by reconstructing the horizontal axis of village or people's power. By doing this the people can free themselves from these hierarchical forces and take charge of their own governance by creating an alternative economic and political system. This is not a recent idea for Sarvodaya, but part of its vision of the awakening process it articulated early on. Sarvodaya has depicted the contrast between the ideal Sarvodaya social order and the present social order with a chart it has published in its literature and displayed in its centers since 1960 (See Figure 5.2).

According to this chart, the "Present Social Order" contrasts with a "Sarvodaya Social Order," because the Present Social Order is characterized by "import-export economy . . . foreign debts, [and] subjugation to neo-colonialism." In such a society, Sarvodaya notes, "the law of enforcement and state power increase, [the] laws of Dharma . . . and power of [the] people diminish. [The] Rulers [are] all powerful and [the] people powerless." By contrast, Sarvodaya's vision of the ideal social order calls for a society based on spiritual values, simplicity, self-sufficiency, decentralization, and people's power. The Sarvodaya Social Order would have "economic resources properly combined . . . [and a] self-sufficient economy based on the primary needs of the people." In such a society, the "Laws of righteousness, strength of Dharma, and power of the people [will] prevail . . . [with] no ruling class, people all powerful,[and] Sarvodaya realized." [22] (See Figure 5.2)

Sarvodaya's rationale for constructing this civil society with a new social order finds a clear mandate in Buddhism, which teaches that a dharmic social order is necessary to provide the context that will enable people to progress toward the goal of enlightenment.

Because Sarvodaya believes that this kind of social transformation is now more possible than ever, its recent thought has reemphasized the Gandhian ideal of gram swaraj. It takes gram swaraj to mean the ability of a village to be self-reliant and to "democratically control and manage its own affairs." [23] Sarvodaya's recent thought once again adheres to the Gandhian idea that a true civilization characterized by qualities such as peace, nonviolence, and liberation can never be created from the top down, but must emerge from the bottom up. As

5.2   Present Social Order/Sarvodaya Social Order.

Present Social Order Nature and Results	**Sarvodaya Social Order** Nature and Results
(1) Absence of self-knowledge and self-reliance.	(1) Striving for self-knowledge and self-reliance.
(2) Blind imitation of materialistic values.	(2) Motivation based on spiritual values rooted in national culture.
(3) Worship of wealth, power, position, untruth, violence, and selfishness dominate.	(3) Respect for virtue, wisdom, capability, truth, non-violence, self-denial dominate.
(4) Organizations based on possessive and competitive instincts become powerful, capitalist economy, bureaucracy, and power and party politics become major social forces.	(4) Organizations based on sharing and co-operation become powerful; social trusteeship economy; people's participation in administration; and party-less people's politics become social realities.
(5) Evil in man is harnessed, society is fragmented through considerations of race, caste, class, religion, party, etc.	(5) Good in man is harnessed, society integrated as one human family.
(6) Economic resources improperly combined, production suffers, unemployment.	(6) Economic resources properly combined, production increases employment.
(7) Import-export economy based on production of commodities inherited from colonial times, foreign debts, subjugation to neo-colonialism.	(7) Self-sufficient economy based on the primary needs of the people, national solvency, national self-respect and economic freedom.
(8) Dependence on large-scale organizations, capital intensive, wastage of human labour, corruption increases, environmental pollution.	(8) Dependence on small-scale organizations, labour-intensive, utilization of human labour, corruption decreases, protection of environment both physical and psychological.
(9) Village subserves the city, rural exodus, moral degeneration, social unrest and stagnation.	(9) Balanced rural and urban awakening, moral regeneration.
(10) Laws of punishment, instruments of law enforcement and state power increase, laws of Dharma, strength of Dharma and power of people diminish. Rulers become all powerful and people powerless.	(10) Laws of righteousness, strength of Dharma and power of the people prevail. No ruling class, people all powerful, Sarvodaya realized.

From. A. T. Ariyaratne, "The Vision of a New Society," (Manila, Philippines: Asian Institute of Management, 1990), 7.

Ariyaratne has said, "Sarvodaya believes that a new social order devoid of present global dangers can only be built if the existing macro socio-economic and political structures can be transformed to serve these [village] levels rather than by being in a position to control them."[24] Sarvodaya's recent programs have the explicit goal of producing villages characterized by this kind of gram swaraj. In its discussion of the stages of village development, Sarvodaya now posits gram swaraj as the sixth or final stage of the Village Graduation Model. For example, in a presentation to its donors in September 2002, Sarvodaya showed an illustration of the five stages of the village graduation process with a large arrow after the fifth stage pointing upward to the goal of gram swaraj. However, if one asks the Sarvodaya leaders how many villages have actually reached this stage, they admit that at present there are very few; but they nevertheless regard it as a viable and necessary goal for village development today.

Facilitating Gram Swaraj

What are the programs that Sarvodaya is currently promoting to realize gram swaraj? How is Sarvodaya working to build up this kind of grassroots autonomy to transform what it sees as the corrupt, centralized, present system and build up a new social order?

Sarvodaya regards some of the programs it has been conducting for years as preparation for gram swaraj. From the beginning, Sarvodaya has approached village development as a process in which the villagers themselves must take ownership. It does not go into a village promising to provide total funding for development, but it assists the residents of a village in organizing shramadanas to address their own problems. As Joanna Macy noted, "To help villagers move out of patterns of apathy and dependence, Movement organizers challenge the villagers, from the moment of the first meeting, to participate in decision making and to take some action—no matter how small or menial—in meeting a local need."[25] This emphasis on local self-reliance is viewed by Sarvodaya as swashakti and janashakti, which represent concrete steps toward gram swaraj.

Sarvodaya continues to promote its list of the Ten Basic Human Needs to provide criteria and goals for sustainable development, and it views this list as an essential part of the groundwork for gram swaraj. The list of basic human needs helps the villagers envision liberating alternatives to the market forces and the consumerist economy. Ariyaratne describes the basic human needs as "targets to be achieved by village communities under their own community leadership."[26] Macy noted that the list serves "to clarify the purposes of a just social order, as well as to set parameters for appropriate consumption and economic enterprise."[27] The basic human needs provide a Buddhist perspective on the goals of development. As Macy said, "These [basic human needs] together with the Buddha's teaching of Right Livelihood set human labor within a context of character formation and life-enhancement that surpasses its worth in terms of income generation alone."[28]

Sarvodaya's preschools represent another long-standing program that it views as laying the groundwork for gram swaraj. As with the shramadanas, Sarvodaya does not intervene in the villages to operate the preschools, but it facilitates the process by which the villagers organize their own preschools. Each village decides how the school should be organized, and each appoints and supports its own teachers. Sarvodaya provides training for the teachers and advice about the curriculum, but the schools operate under village control. In this sense they represent an exercise in village self-determination. Ariyaratne sees the preschools as one step toward transcending the present system. He notes that, even with the first school at Kanatoluwa, the villagers were changing the system, because the government opposed having a school in the village; but once it was started, the government had to accept it.[29]

The peace meditations represent the means to generate and demonstrate the peoples' consciousness of the need for liberation and self-determination. Although their primary purpose is to create a spirit of peace in the country, they also provide a vehicle for the people to fight back against the entire centralized system that is causing the suffering at the village level. In this sense, the peace meditations serve a very important purpose in the preparation for gram swaraj.

One of the key programs in Sarvodaya's scheme to achieve gram swaraj is its village banking program administered by SEEDS. In 2002 there were 670 Sarvodaya village banks and over three thousand villages with SEEDS-supported economic programs. Sarvodaya's village banks and credit societies, like its preschools, are administered and governed by the people in the villages. Liberating the people from the centralized banking system, the village banks provide economic empowerment and self reliance to prepare the people for gram swaraj. To build on the success of the village banks, Sarvodaya planned to establish a Sarvodaya Development Bank that would constitute an apex bank linking all of the village banks. SEEDS explained that it "has laid the foundation for a village-banking infrastructure that mobilises rural capital and uses it for rural benefit."[30] Sarvodaya projected that by 2003, this Sarvodaya

Development Bank would serve almost five hundred thousand people with loans and have savings of over Rs 1 billion, making it one of the most powerful banks in the country.[31] Having a Development Bank will make the Sarvodaya Movement as a whole more self-sustaining and will free its banking program from a partial dependence on government and commercial banks.

According to the director of SEEDS, the Development Bank will change the economic order of the country by bringing bottom-up banking and fostering sustainable development.[32] Sarvodaya expects that the economic liberation that results from this transformation of the banking system will further prepare the people to transform the political system and the other centralized systems that oppress them. Sarvodaya's village banking system serves as a concrete example of how its reforms that begin in the village can rise to impact the national level as the grassroots network acquires power.

Information technology (IT) represents another area that Sarvodaya is emphasizing as a vehicle for gram swaraj. Technology was one of the three points accented in Sarvodaya's strategic plan for 2000–05 (along with spirituality and politics) as keys to attaining social health.[33] Sarvodaya is working to make information technology available to the villages through village and regional "telecenters" that will provide telephone, e-mail, and computer facilities. These centers will offer IT training for rural youth and adults. In addition, these district telecenters will be used as business promotion centers in connection with the SEEDS banks. At this time, Sarvodaya has four regional telecenters—in Moratuwa, Ratnapura, Kulupitya, and Anuradhapura—staffed by trained IT instructors. In addition to expanding the number of these centers, Sarvodaya also plans to launch a mobile multimedia unit that will travel to remote villages to provide IT instruction and access. In this effort, Sarvodaya has enlisted the cooperation of Sri Lanka's Council for Information Technology (CINTEC), the Institute for Computer Technology, and the University of Moratuwa.

The goal of this scheme is to link the villages electronically, which will enable them to compete with the established centralized economic and political systems. Sarvodaya seeks to use technology to create the kind of informal informational networks that David Korten and others have described as essential for "people centered development."[34] Ariyaratne hopes that this will help reconstruct the horizontal axis of the villages. "My answer is the vision of highly decentralized communities in the world getting networked together and bypassing the centers of power."[35] Sarvodaya reasons "that the new global information technologies can be useful not only for economic purposes,

such as market identification and communication, but also for democratic self-governance. For isolated villages to network effectively, they
must have access to communication as well as up to the minute news of
current events. Only then can they participate effectively in an environment that favours urban concentrations of political power."[36]

Two other programs that Sarvodaya was emphasizing in 2002 have
significance for the Movement's goal of fostering gram swaraj. The first
is the *Nagarodaya,* or Urban Awakening Program, which represents a
crucial step on the road to gram swaraj. In 2002 Sarvodaya established
a new Nagarodaya Center in Colombo to extend the development programs that it traditionally facilitated in the rural areas to the urban community. Although it has had a small urban program for several years, the
new Nagarodaya Center will enable Sarvodaya to offer greater assistance to the urban poor, many of whom have migrated to the city from
village areas in search of better opportunities.

Sarvodaya's Nagarodaya Center is a modern, five-story facility located
near one of the city's poorest areas. It offers various services to the people
in Colombo, including a telecenter similar to the ones Sarvodaya is establishing in the villages, a community health institute, an auditorium and
training center, and a child development resource center. Sarvodaya envisions that the community health institute and the technology center will
become hubs for its national programs in urban areas. The Nagarodaya
Center represents the Movement's recognition that it must assist the urban
community as well as the rural, if it hopes to build a just society and bring
social and economic reform on a national scale.

The second program is the Five R's Program (Relief, Rehabilitation,
Reconciliation, Reconstruction, and Reawakening). As the ethnic conflict has entered a period of peace negotiations (since 2002), it has
become possible for Sarvodaya and other NGOs to resume and expand
their work in the northern and eastern parts of the country. Sarvodaya
has a great opportunity to shape the process of rehabilitation and rede-
velopment in these areas. By assisting the people to rebuild these war-
ravaged villages, Sarvodaya can help the people in these areas begin to
move toward gram swaraj. Given the current conditions in the north
and east, however, gram swaraj represents a distant goal for those
villages, but the advent of peaceful conditions provides an opportunity
to begin the process of village awakening that can lead to it.

Although Sarvodaya's leaders hope they can decentralize the process of
development to the villages by enabling villages throughout the country to
reach gram swaraj, the north and east will require a lengthy period of assistance before these villages will be self-reliant. For this reason, these areas
will necessarily constitute a key focus for the Movement for many years.

Power: Deshodaya

The third element of the triad that Sarvodaya has deemed essential for social health is power, specifically, political power. In Sarvodaya's more recent discourse, this element is expressed in terms of deshodaya. For Sarvodaya, deshodaya represents the logical extension of gram swaraj to the national level. Sarvodaya envisions a process of political liberation, beginning from the grass roots, that parallels and builds upon the economic liberation that it has begun with the village banks. This political liberation would complete Sarvodaya's strategy for reform and provide the means for actualizing a Sarvodaya Social Order. Deshodaya has always been part of Sarvodaya's theory of how awakening proceeds from the individual to the global level, but now Sarvodaya has come to regard it as not only a necessary, but also an attainable goal. As Sarvodaya's leaders recognize, however, deshodaya will be the most difficult element of the triad to accomplish; many questions surround both the meaning of the concept and the ways to actualize it.

Ariyaratne defines deshodaya in terms of the kind of Gandhian system of participatory democracy that he has advocated for many years. He said, "The essence of Deshodaya is the real exercise of power by relatively small rural and urban communities through the selection of community-level representatives . . . answerable directly to the communities themselves."[37] For deshodaya to come about, Sarvodaya reiterates that the current party political system must be changed. Sarvodaya describes the kind of reform needed as a transition from the current situation where "power is in the hands of elites and ordinary people are powerless to change their lives" to a situation with power concentrated at the "lowest possible level" through village self-determination (see Figure 5.1).

To achieve deshodaya, Sarvodaya proposes to actualize the consensus political system that Ariyaratne has advocated. That Sarvodaya has decided to attempt to make this Gandhian political ideal a reality is a sign of their frustration with the conditions in the country. It is also a sign of Sarvodaya's evolution and growth; Sarvodaya now feels it can institute its own system and accomplish what the government has been unable to accomplish. Ariyaratne points out that Sarvodaya has already taken programs that benefit the people, such as education and banking, from the grass roots to the national level. At the same time, however, "the government has pursued a top-down policy of war, development, and [attempts at] peace that has led to destruction. The power of the higher levels was held by political parties that came and went. All power was held and acted on by few people from the towns. The people at the village who should have democratic rights only had the right to make their vote every five years.

Due to the party and power hungry political system, from the family to the nation, the people were divided."[38]

Acting to counter this system, Sarvodaya has established a Deshodaya Organization that is working to foster grassroots political reform. The organization was founded in 2001 as a subsidiary organization to the Sarvodaya Movement. Among the goals of the "Deshodaya Path" as listed in the booklet, *Rules of Deshodaya,* are: changing the political structure of the country by "the creation of a consensual political culture, devoid of political party differences"; and enacting "a new constitution" that will establish such a system.[39]

When Sarvodaya announced the formation of the Deshodaya Organization, the government media and Sarvodaya's opponents immediately described it as a new political party. Sarvodaya's leaders rejected this description, saying that the Movement had no intention of entering the party political system, because it intends to abolish that system. Nevertheless, the media and many of Sarvodaya's own supporters have tended to view deshodaya as Sarvodaya's entry into politics. At the October 2002 annual meeting of the Deshodaya Organization, several speakers expressed the hope that A. T. Ariyaratne would run for president of the country. In an interview, a Sarvodaya leader explained his view of deshodaya and concluded by saying that "the ultimate outcome should be for Dr. Ariyaratne to come forward to be president."

People outside the Movement also have the impression that deshodaya represents Ariyaratne's entry into politics. When asked what they thought deshodaya meant, Muslim informants said that "most Muslims believe Ariyaratne is trying to campaign for office somewhat through the backdoor." They went on to say, however, that if "the people see that Sarvodaya is doing good for the country, they will support deshodaya."[40] For his part, Ariyaratne says he is not running for president, but—as he has done in the past—he leaves open the possibility that he would "come forward" if the people in a consensus system requested him to serve.

In presenting deshodaya to the public, Sarvodaya's leaders have invoked again the Gandhian and Buddhist ideals of participatory democracy. Ariyaratne said, for example, "The Buddhist vision of a country ruled by *dasa rāja dhammā* or the ten principles of good governance can easily be realized if we adopt the Deshodaya programme that is being offered to the nation by Sarvodaya. This is on the same lines as the ancient Buddhist Republics of Licchavis and Vajjis and Mahatma Gandhi's concept of village republics." He also compares the system of deshodaya to the rule of Ashoka.[41] Sarvodaya's leaders refer to the Gandhian panchayat ideal and the ancient Buddhist republics for the same reason that Ariyaratne has referred to them in previous years: to provide authoritative models to counter the dominant Western political and economic model. The leaders recognize that these Gandhian and Buddhist models have been highly romanticized and cannot be taken literally, however, it is not always clear that their followers also recognize this. In addition, although the references to ancient Buddhist republics may be persuasive to Buddhists, such references do not seem to support Sarvodaya's goal of ecumenicity, and carry little weight with non-Buddhists.

Sarvodaya explains that deshodaya will result when a critical mass of villages reaches the stage of gram swaraj and the people move to take charge of their own political destiny. Although there is logic to this scenario, the problem is that at present very few villages have reached the stage of gram swaraj, nor do they have the requisite autonomy to demand self-governance. Ariyaratne does not see these as a barrier, however; his earlier millennial predictions figure into his calculus for deshodaya as he argues that the realization of deshodaya—and gram swaraj—can also happen very quickly if the prevailing system crashes. He now believes that the collapse of the present system will occur in stages, beginning from the present when there is already increased crime and large-scale corruption. When the scope of corruption and crime becomes too great, Ariyaratne believes the people will revolt and overthrow the present political and economic systems. Ariyaratne makes the comparison to the Berlin Wall, saying that "no one expected the wall would come down, but it did. Similarly, in Sri Lanka if enough people become disenchanted with the present system, changes could come quickly here too."[42] When this occurs, Ariyaratne believes that the people will turn to Sarvodaya, because they recognize the value of developing nonviolent and sustainable communities, instead of supporting a violent, dictatorial system.

In sum, how viable is this ideal of deshodaya? Clearly, deshodaya represents a difficult and somewhat romantic goal. As part of Sarvodaya's programmatic vision, however, deshodaya has both long-term and short-term implications. In the long term, accomplishing deshodaya would mean the realization of Sarvodaya's vision of a Sarvodaya social order and a civil society. As Ariyaratne said, "Under Deshodaya we are expecting to expand the decision making area of the communities so that it covers all of their life. . . . We believe that under Deshodaya there will be lasting peace and harmony in the country."[43]

Unless Ariyaratne's millennial predictions are right, however, and something like the fall of the Berlin Wall happens in Sri Lanka, the attainment of this kind of national awakening will require a long and

difficult process. Attempting to realize this goal will also involve Sarvodaya in politics, even if they have in mind the goal of establishing a new
political paradigm. The following excerpt from an editorial in the *Daily
Mirror* accepts Sarvodaya's right to engage in politics, but also points
out some of the difficulties of Sarvodaya's path by connecting Sarvodaya's aspirations for deshodaya with the problems of the 2002 Kandy
peace meditation.

> "As to why some have raised objections to Sarvodaya form-
> ing a political party, [it] is unfathomable. When small groups
> of people with petty policies and purposes are transforming
> themselves into political parties and attempting to pose as
> major national parties, what indeed withholds the Sarvodaya
> movement with considerable backing from people through-
> out the country and with a record of impressive service to the
> people from launching a political party? Paradoxical though
> it may seem, the new party, Deshodaya's policy is to unite
> people through consensual politics to make this country
> a granary. Though it seeks to educate people on non-
> confrontational politics, how difficult it is to practise this
> policy probably became clear to them when they had to con-
> tend with the confrontation that they faced in Kandy last
> week." [44]

But even if the long-term goal of actualizing deshodaya is remote,
Sarvodaya's emphasis on this ideal may have short-term benefits. By
addressing this issue and creating a new organization within Sarvodaya,
the leaders of Sarvodaya may be able to recapture some of the original
spirit of the Movement. This would be important, since much of that
original spirit seems to have been eroded when Sarvodaya became a
large NGO. Today, many people in Sarvodaya talk about the need to
rekindle this "movement spirit," and it is likely that Ariyaratne had this
in mind when he proposed the deshodaya emphasis. If Sarvodaya can
rekindle the movement spirit in the short term, that will help it make
progress toward realizing the long-term goal of full deshodaya. The road
to deshodaya is undoubtedly long and difficult, but since Sarvodaya has
always aimed high and has had amazing success, one should not rule out
anything.

EPILOGUE

VISHVODAYA, WORLD AWAKENING

Ultimately, Sarvodaya proposes to go beyond deshodaya, to vishvodaya, world awakening. This aim prompts questions about what role Sarvodaya can play in the global arena. Can its program of awakening be applied in cultures outside of Sri Lanka? Does its form of socially engaged Buddhism offer solutions for the problems of the non-Buddhist world also? What contribution can the evolving Sarvodaya Movement make to the emerging global dialogue on economics, politics, and spiritual awakening? Sarvodaya clearly has much to contribute to this dialogue, especially in the area of conflict resolution and peace. Sarvodaya is to be commended for standing up for peace in a South Asian region that has been wracked by conflict and violence in recent years. Sarvodaya has been one of the few voices in that region actively calling for peace and seeking to build a consensus for peace.

The world can clearly benefit from Sarvodaya's message of peace from a Buddhist perspective. As our globe becomes smaller and the competition between nations and groups becomes more intense, people need to hear Sarvodaya's interpretation of the Buddhist teachings about the interconnectedness of all beings. These teachings provide an essential antidote to the forces of globalization and Westernization that tend to emphasize individualism and competition, thus elevating human desire to the status of a virtue. Drawing on its Buddhist and Gandhian heritage, Sarvodaya has shown that this materialistic philosophy based on desire creates structures of violence that lead the world away from peace and closer to social and environmental destruction.

As the Sarvodaya Movement evolves, it hopes to address these issues on both the national and the international levels. As it is able to promote village self-reliance, Sarvodaya plans to devolve more power and responsibility to the villages and the district centers. This will enable the Sarvodaya headquarters to focus on education, policy research, and advocacy on national and international issues. With the emergence of new leadership in Sarvodaya, this kind of transition is already underway.

The current Executive Director, Dr. Vinya Ariyaratne, has begun to change Sarvodaya's national role from one of a development agency to one of a clearinghouse for information on matters such as appropriate technology, community health, and peace. Since deshodaya and establishing self-reliant villages remain somewhat distant goals, however, it will take some time for Sarvodaya to complete this kind of transformation; it will have to continue many of the current development programs for an indefinite period.

Even now, while Sarvodaya's new role is evolving, the organization is establishing an international presence. Sarvodaya has a number of international groups that support its activities and seek to apply its insights. These include Sarvodaya USA, Sarvodaya Twente in the Netherlands, Sarvodaya Japan, and Sarvodaya UK. Sarvodaya USA represents the oldest and largest of these international groups, all of which actively support the Movement by raising funds and attempting to adapt Sarvodaya's programs for new contexts. In addition, Sarvodaya has formed alliances with other like-minded international organizations. It carries out projects and engages in dialogue with these groups. These links include groups such as Friends Without A Border, which operates the Angkor Hospital for Children in Cambodia; One World One People in Japan; the Global Eco-Village Network that is headquartered in Denmark; and the Commonway Institute in Portland, Oregon.

Through networking with these groups and through other means, Sarvodaya can engage in the international dialogue about the global predicament and its possible solutions. David Korten described the nature of this predicament saying, "Our relentless pursuit of economic growth is accelerating the breakdown of the planet's life support systems, intensifying resource competition, widening the gap between rich and poor, and undermining the values and relationships of family and community."[1] He also expressed a millennial vision that resonates with that of Sarvodaya: "[W]e are experiencing accelerating social and environmental disintegration in nearly every country of the world—as revealed by a rise in poverty, unemployment, inequality, violent crime, failing families, and environmental degradation."[2] Ariyaratne's similar predictions about the disintegration of the economic and political superstructure and the impact of this on the lives of the people have highlighted the gravity of this problem for the people of Sri Lanka and the world.

But if Korten and Ariyaratne share a diagnosis of the predicament, they along with others also share a vision of a solution. This solution takes the form of a new paradigm that is emerging in the world to bring revolutionary social change. Willis Harman characterized this new paradigm as one in which "increased emphasis is placed on humanistic and spiritual values, quality of life, community, person-centered society . . . [and where] emphasis on materialistic values, status goals, and unqualified economic growth is diminished."[3] Similarly, Alvin Toffler calls this new paradigm a "Third Wave" and predicted that it will transform all aspects of human existence:

> "The Third Wave brings with it a genuinely new way of life based on diversified, renewable energy sources; on methods of production that make most factory assembly lines obsolete; on new non-nuclear families; on a novel institution that might be called the 'electronic cottage'; and on radically changed schools and corporations of the future. The emergent civilization writes a new code of behavior for us and carries us beyond standardization, synchronization, and centralization, beyond the concentration of energy, money, and power."[4]

Korten cited Thomas Berry as another voice who "argues eloquently in *Dream of the Earth* that our future depends on a new cosmic story that restores sacred meaning to life and draws us to explore life's still-unrealized potentials." He also noted that "such a story is taking shape and drawing inspiration from many sources, including findings from the modern physical and life sciences and the world's richly varied spiritual traditions."[5] This new paradigm is necessary to deal with the new challenges of the postcolonial and postindustrial age. As Korten noted, the approach to development in this new age "must be guided by a new paradigm based on alternative ideas, values, social technique, and technology."[6] Clearly Sarvodaya, with its over four decades of experience and thought about the nature of grassroots development, has been one of the pioneers in the articulation of this new paradigm.

In 2002, during a conversation in Moratuwa, Ariyaratne explained that the reason Sarvodaya is trying to facilitate deshodaya is that Sri Lanka is a small country with limited resources; it must find sustainable ways to live within its limits. By contrast, he said, rich nations either have more resources of their own or have the power to seize the resources of other nations to meet their needs, so they do not have the same problems as small nations.[7] Although what Ariyaratne said is undoubtedly accurate as a description of the current situation and the short term, in the long term all nations and all people are in the same situation as Sri Lanka. We must all find sustainable approaches to living with limited resources on "Spaceship Earth." It is in this regard that Sarvodaya's insights can enrich the global dialogue by sharing the Movement's experience.

Korten discussed a number of themes that he sees as essential for the new development paradigm, and many of these represent themes that Sarvodaya has already applied in its work. Korten contrasted "production-centered development" with "people-centered development," and said that the success of the new paradigm depends on the emergence of "the alternative ideas, values, social techniques, and technologies of people-centered development. The creation of such alternatives presents an important and immediate human challenge."[8] Clearly Sarvodaya has ample experience with "people-centered development," and has created many alternative approaches to this kind of development, that it can share with others. Korten also discussed a number of examples of people who have fought back against the prevailing capitalist system. He cited Barlow, who said, "We must not accept the prevailing propaganda that globalization and corporate rule are inevitable," and observed that, "we are in the midst of fundamentally new phenomenon in the modern human experience, the creation of a new civilization from the bottom up."[9] Again, this is an area of strength for Sarvodaya; the Movement can share with others its approaches to bottom-up development in many areas, such as education and banking.

Perhaps the most important theme that Sarvodaya can contribute to the global dialogue, however, is its emphasis on a development based on spirituality and a spiritual consciousness. Although Sarvodaya has sought a balanced development that integrates social, economic, political, and spiritual elements, the key to its system is the spiritual element. Korten also argued for the significance of the spiritual, saying, "I believe that the task ahead depends even more on our spiritual awakening than on our political awakening. . . ."[10] He also expanded on his belief in this statement:

> "I believe that we have access to an inner spiritual wisdom and that our collective salvation as a species depends in part on tapping into this wisdom from which the institutions of modern science, the market, and even religion have deeply alienated us. Through this rediscovery we may achieve the creative balance between market and community, science and religion, and money and spirit that is essential to the creation and maintenance of healthy human societies."[11]

Ariyaratne and Sarvodaya concur. Sarvodaya's massive peace meditations have been predicated on the idea that generating a critical mass of spiritual consciousness represents the key to achieving peace. But

Sarvodaya does not view peace as an isolated goal; rather, it believes that true peace will only come as part of a nonviolent revolution that transforms the society, the economy, and the polity, and reforms the values and the structures that create conflict. An awakened spiritual consciousness represents the key to this kind of social revolution. In this sense, Sarvodaya can speak to the recent emphasis on "faith-based initiatives." Sarvodaya has much to say about the nature and meaning of such initiatives based on its years of experience in implementing its programs in Sri Lanka. Sarvodaya's Buddhist perspectives on these issues of how to awaken and assist the poorest of the poor can enrich the global dialogue on religion and social liberation. Sarvodaya represents a remarkable example of a spiritual movement that seeks social justice, development, and a total social revolution.

Although Sarvodaya's ideas for a nonviolent revolution and a transformed society may appear utopian to some, they are utopian in a positive and prophetic sense. They point to other and more ideal alternatives to the violent paradigm of global materialism and consumerism that threatens to undermine cultural values and bring chaos on both the social and environmental planes.[12] Sarvodaya invokes Gandhian and Buddhist spiritual values not in order to return to the past or to build up a Buddhist identity, but to orient society toward these ideals of spirituality, equality, simplicity, and conservation. Sarvodaya has taught countless individuals how to awaken themselves to these spiritual values by working to awaken their communities.

In the international forum, Sarvodaya can share its understanding of these Gandhian and Buddhist ideals that apply to a new paradigm for development. Sarvodaya's view of a global civil society and the growing gap between the rich and poor, for example, has been informed by Gandhi's views of wealth and poverty. Gandhi noted that people will never be able to live in peace as long as some are living in palaces and others in slums. He said the poor "will have no recourse but to resort to both violence and untruth."[13] Sarvodaya has sought to address these issues in order to build an infrastructure for peace and holistic social health. From Gandhian and Buddhist sources, Sarvodaya affirms Schumacher's ideal of "Small is Beautiful," and seeks to transform the values motivating society today.

To summarize the kind of socially engaged Buddhist vision that Sarvodaya might offer in the global dialogue on the meaning of development, we can refer to a statement made by a contemporary Thai Buddhist reformer, Sulak Sivaraksa. Sivaraksa has similarly endeavored to use Buddhist values to rectify the structural violence created by Western capitalist development. He said,

"Economists measure development in terms of increasing currency and material items, thus fostering greed. Politicians see development in terms of increased power, fostering hatred. Both measure the results strictly in terms of quantity, fostering delusion. From the Buddhist point of view, development must aim at the reduction of these three poisons—greed, hatred, and delusion, not at their increase. We must develop our spirit."[14]

NOTES

Introduction
A Dharmic Vision for Society

1. Peter L. Berger, "Secularism in Retreat," *National Interest* 46 (Winter 96/97), 3.

2. Max Weber, *The Religion of India* (trans. H. Gerth and D. Martindale) (New York: The Free Press, 1958), 215.

3. "An Endowment Fund for the Sarvodaya Shramadana Movement," (Sarvodaya document, November 1996), 2.

4. Detlef Kantowsky, *Sarvodaya: The Other Development* (New Delhi: Vikas Publishing House, 1980), 142.

5. A. T. Ariyaratne, *In Search of Development* (Moratuwa: Sarvodaya Press, 1982), 1.

6. Denis Goulet, *Survival with Integrity: Sarvodaya at the Crossroads* (Colombo, Sri Lanka: Marga Institute, 1981) 1ff.

7. From a speech to the Central Bank of Ceylon, July 20, 1994.

8. David C. Korten, *When Corporations Rule the World* (West Hartford, CT: Kumarian Press, and San Francisco: Berrett-Koehler Publishers, 1995), 14.

9. A. T. Ariyaratne, Acceptance Speech for the Niwano Peace Prize, 1992. (Moratuwa: Sarvodaya Vishva Lekha Press, 1992), 4.

Chapter One
The Origin and Evolution of the Vision and the Movement

1. A. T. Ariyaratne, "The Sarvodaya Shramadana Movement: Hundred Village Development Scheme," (1970) in *Collected Works,* Vol. I, first edition (Moratuwa: Sarvodaya Press, n. d.), 55.

2. Ibid., 57.

3. Ibid.

4. Ibid.

5. *Sarvodaya, Its Many Facets: the Movement* (Moratuwa: Sarvodaya Press, 1996), 3.

6. Bond, George D., "A.T. Ariyaratne and the Sarvodaya Shramadana Movement in Sri Lanka," in Christopher S. Queen and Sallie B. King (eds.), *Engaged Buddhism: Buddhist Liberation Movements in Asia* (Albany, NY: State University of New York Press, 1996) 122–124 and 126.

7. Nandasena Ratnapala, *Sarvodaya in Sri Lanka* (Moratuwa: Sarvodaya Publications, 1978), 6.

8. M. K. Gandhi, *Young India* (December 20, 1928), 420.

9. M. K. Gandhi, *Young India* (September 3, 1925), 304.

10. Cited in Hans Wismeijer's *Diversity in Harmony* (A privately published dissertation from the Department of Cultural Anthropology, University of Utrecht, Netherlands, 1981), 33.

11. Detlef Kantowsky, *Sarvodaya: The Other Development*, 8.

12. Ibid., 10.

13. *Sarvodaya Shramadana: Growth of a People's Movement* (Sarvodaya booklet, 1974), 11.

14. Joanna Macy, *Dharma and Development: Religion as a Resource in the Sarvodaya Self-Help Movement* (West Hartford, CT: Kumarian Press, 1983), 32.

15. Ananda Guruge, *Return to Righteousness* (Colombo: Government Press, 1965), 737.

16. Ibid., 337.

17. Ibid., 748.

18. Ibid., 339.

19. Ibid., 489.

20. Detlef Kantowsky, *Sarvodaya: The Other Development*, 186.

21. Ibid., 44.

22. Ibid., 190.

23. Richard Gombrich and Gananath Obeyesekere, *Buddhism Transformed* (Princeton, NJ: Princeton University Press, 1988), 248.

24. Detlef Kantowsky, *Sarvodaya: The Other Development*, 182.

25. "Words Together with Action," "Sarvodaya Newspaper," April, 1961, cited in *The Power Pyramid and Dharmic Cycle* (Ratmalana: Sarvodaya Vishva Lekha Press, 1988), 32.

26. "Living with Religion in the Midst of Violence," *Bulletin of Peace Proposals* 21:3 (1990), 282.

27. A. T. Ariyaratne, *The Power Pyramid and the Dharmic Cycle* 177. See also 108 where he says, "By the term 'religion' I do not mean a particular religion or religions. I would analyse the term 'religion' to mean any spiritual nature that is prevalent at any stage among the people."

28. Wismeijer, *Diversity in Harmony,* 41.

29. *The Power Pyramid and the Dharmic Cycle,* 177.

30. Interview in *Dana,* Vol. XVII, Nos. 11–12 (Nov.–Dec. 1992), 16.

31. Joanna Macy, *Dharma and Development,* 30.

32. Detlef Kantowsky, *Sarvodaya: The Other Development,* 75.

33. A. T. Ariyaratne, "Sarvodaya Shramadana Movement: Hundred Villages Development Scheme," in *Collected Works,* Vol. I, 47.

34. "A People's Agenda for Global Awakening," Ninth Niwano Peace Prize Ceremony (1992), 3.

35. A. T. Ariyaratne, *Collected Works,* Vol. I, 133.

36. Joanna Macy, *Dharma and Development,* 37.

37. A. T. Ariyaratne, *In Search of Development,* 16.

38. *Dana,* Vol. XIV, no. 9 (1989), 13.

39. See *Basic Human Needs: A Framework for Action,* John McHale and Magda McHale. (A Report to the UN Environment Program) (Transaction Books: 1978), 12ff. Also *The Planetary Bargain: Proposals for a New International Economic Order to Meet Human Needs* (A policy paper of the Aspen Institute for Humanistic Studies, 1975).

40. This list is discussed in Ariyaratne, *Collected Works,* Vol. II (Sarvodaya Research Institute,1981), 80.

41. A. T. Ariyaratne, "Gandhi Peace Prize Acceptance Speech," January 1, 1997, 14.

42. Detlef Kantowsky, *Sarvodaya: The Other Development,* 61.

43. A. T. Ariyaratne, *Collected Works,* Vol. II, 81.

44. Ariyaratne, *Collected Works,* Vol. IV, (Ratmalana, Sri Lanka: Sarvodaya Vishva Lekha Press, 1989), 37

45. A. T. Ariyaratne, *Collected Works,* Vol. I, 58.

46. Winston King, *In the Hope of Nibbana* (LaSalle, Ill.: Open Court Press, 1964), 183.

47. A. T. Ariyaratne, *Collected Works*, Vol. II, 49.

48. A. T. Ariyaratne, *Collected Works*, Vol. I, 119.

49. Joanna Macy, *Dharma and Development*, 52.

50. *Sarvodaya Shramadana: Growth of a People's Movement*, (Sarvodaya, 1974), 17.

51. This comment was made during an interview in August 1997.

52. A. T. Ariyaratne, *Collected Works*, Vol. II, 84.

53. Detlef Kantowsky, *Sarvodaya: The Other Development*, 166.

54. Joanna Macy, *Dharma and Development*, 58.

55. A. T. Ariyaratne, *Sarvodaya and Development*, (Moratuwa: Sarvodaya Press, 1979), 12.

56. *Ethos and Work Plan* (Moratuwa: Sarvodaya Press, n.d. circa 1977), 25.

57. Ibid., 46.

58. Joanna Macy, *Dharma and Development*, 81.

59. Ibid., 86.

60. A. T. Ariyaratne and D. A. Perera, *Sarvodaya as a Movement*, (Moratuwa: Sarvodaya Press, 1989), 6.

61. Joanna Macy, *"World as Love, World as Self* (Berkeley, CA: Parallax Press, 1991), 81.

62. A. T. Ariyaratne, "The Sarvodaya Shramadana Movement: Hundred Village Development Scheme," in *Collected Works*, Vol. I, 73.

63. One foundation was the Netherlands Organization for International Development (NOVIB) and the other was F.A.I.M.

64. A. T. Ariyaratne, D. A. Perera, *Sarvodaya as a Movement*, (Moratuwa: Sarvodaya Press, 1989), 4.

65. See Sjef Theunis, "Years of Critical Brotherhood," *Anjali Pranam* (A felicitation volume for A. T. Ariyaratne), (Moratuwa: Sarvodaya Publishing, 1980).

66. Nandsena Ratnapala, *Study Service in the Sarvodaya Shramadana Movement in Sri Lanka, 1958–1976* (Colombo: Sarvodaya Research Centre, 1976), 109.

67. A. T. Ariyaratne, "Sarvodaya Shramadana Movement: Towards a Global Perspective from a Rural Experience," in *Collected Works*, Vol. II, 83.

Chapter Two
Sarvodaya's Vision of Peace in a Context of Violence

1. *Peace Making in Sri Lanka in the Buddhist Context*, (Ratmalana, Sri Lanka: Sarvodaya Vishva Lekha Press, 1987), 6.

2. The Janatha Vimukti Peramuna (JVP) started as a Sinhala nationalistic and socialistic movement and unsuccessfully tried to overthrow the government in 1971 and again in 1989.

3. Acariya Buddharakkhita, *The Dhammapada: The Buddha's Path of Wisdom*, verses 1–2 (Kandy, Sri Lanka: Buddhist Publication Society, 1985). I have used the Pali verses from this edition of the *Dhammapada*, but have provided my own translation which differs in some places.

4. *Dīgha Nikāya* Vol. I, .(London: Pali Text Society, 1947), 73.

5. I. B. Horner (trans.), *The Middle Length Sayings (Majjhima-Nikaya)* (London: Pali Text Society, 1954), 160.

6. *Dhammapada*, verse 5.

7. *Dhammapada*, verses 3–4.

8. *Dhammapada*, verse 201.

9. A. T. Ariyaratne, "What To Do?" from Detlef Kantowsky, *Learning How to Live in Peace* (Ratmalana, Sri Lanka: Sarvodaya Vishva Lekha Press, 1987), 16f.

10. *Peace Making in Sri Lanka in the Buddhist Context*, 14.

11. Cited by Samudhu Weerawarne, "Dr. A. T. Ariyaratne At Close Quarters," in *People's Peace Initiative* (Ratmalana, Sri Lanka: Sarvodaya Vishva Lekha Press), 31.

12. A. T. Ariyaratne, "Five Lessons and a Goal," *Collected Works* Vol. IV, 120.

13. *Peace Making in Sri Lanka in the Buddhist Context*, 1.

14. Joanna Macy, *Dharma and Development*, 32.

15. Ibid., 32

16. At that time, 24% of the Sarvodaya villages were located in the north and east. Detlef Kantowsky, *Learning How to Live in Peace* , 9.

17. The full text of this document is given in A. T. Ariyaratne, *Collected Works*, Vol. III (Ratmalana, Sri Lanka: Sarvodaya Vishva Lekha Press, 1985), 174–195. It was also published as a separate document.

18. Detlef Kantowsky, "Learning How to Live in Peace: The Savrodaya Shramadana Movement of Sri Lanka," in Detlef Kantowsky (ed.), *Learning How to Live in Peace* (Ratmalana, Sri Lanka: Sarvodaya Vishva Lekha Press, n.d.), 1.

19. *Peace Making in Sri Lanka in the Buddhist Context,* 11.

20. Ibid.

21. A. T. Ariyaratne, *The Power Pyramid and the Dharmic Cycle,* 147.

22. *Peace Making in Sri Lanka in the Buddhist Context,* 12.

23. A. T. Ariyaratne, *Power Pyramid and the Dharmic Cycle,* 147.

24. Ibid., 149.

25. *People's Declaration for National Peace and Harmony* (Conference document, "Adopted at the conclusion of the General Conference, October, 1 and 2, 1983"), 15.

26. Ibid., 17.

27. Ibid., 18.

28. A. T. Ariyaratne, *Power Pyramid and the Dharmic Cycle,* 147.

29. *People's Declaration for National Peace and Harmony,* 21.

30. Ibid., 30.

31. Most people seemed to understand why Ariyaratne had to stop the peace march. However, some were critical of his capitulation to the president. One university lecturer accused Ariyaratne of losing his nerve. He said, "He pretends to be like Gandhi, but we know what Gandhi would have done."(Interview, Colombo, June 27, 1985).

32. Speech delivered on September 26, 1986 at the "Peace Walk Ceremony in Vavuniya on behalf of Mr. K. Kadiramalai," *Dana,* Vol. XI, Nos. 10–11, 26.

33. A. T. Ariyaratne, *Power Pyramid and the Dharmic Cycle,* 163.

34. *Peace Making in Sri Lanka in the Buddhist Context,* 16.

35. "Sarvodaya Annual Report," 1992–93, 43.

36. "Sarvodaya Strategic Plan," 1991–94, 10.

37. "Sarvodaya Annual Report," 1992–93, 44.

38. The Liberation Tigers of Tamil Eelam is the main Tamil insurgent group that has been fighting the government and trying to establish its own homeland in the northern and eastern parts of Sri Lanka.

39. "Jaffna Welcomes You," *Daily News,* October 23, 1997.

40. Gandhi Peace Prize presentation booklet, 2.

41. Niwano Peace Prize, "Acceptance Speech," December 1992, 20.

42. Gandhi Peace Prize, "Acceptance Speech," January 1, 1997, 7.

43. *Peace Making in Sri Lanka in the Buddhist Context*, 2.

44. *Daily News*, March 1, 1992. Also see Jehan Perera, C. Marasinghe, and L. Jayasekera, *A People's Movement Under Siege* (Sarvodaya Press, 1992), 199.

45. Brochure, "Vishva Niketan, Universal Abode, A Dream Becoming a Reality" (Sarvodaya, 1998).

46. Ibid.

47. "Towards Peace, Right Livelihood, and Community Self Governance, a Five Year Comprehensive Plan for the Sarvodaya Shramadana Movement 2000–2005," 57f.

48. Gandhi Peace Prize, "Acceptance Speech," 1997, 12.

49. "Sarvodaya Annual Report," 1992–93, 48.

50. D. J. Mitchell, "Why war? A brief analysis of the Sri Lankan Conflict," cited in *People's Peace Initiative,* (Sarvodaya Press, 2000), 11.

51. Gandhi Peace Prize "Acceptance Speech," 1997, 12.

52. "The Solution to Continuing War: An Overview of the Sarvodaya People's Peace Plan" (circa 1999). This document also appeared on the Sarvodaya Web site, www.sarvodaya.org, in 2001, 2–3.

53. Ibid., 1.

54. Ibid., 6.

55. Joanna Macy, "The Sound of Bombs *not* Exploding," *Yes!* (Summer 2002), 53.

56. Ibid., 54.

57. "The Solution to Continuing War: An Overview of the Sarvodaya People's Peace Plan." (Sarvodaya, 1999), 8f.

58. "Towards Peace, Right Livelihood and Community Self-Governance, A Five year Comprehensive Plan for the Sarvodaya Shramadana Movement, 2000–2005" (internal Sarvodaya document), 58.

59. A. T. Ariyaratne, *The Power Pyramid and the Dharmic Cycle*, 37.

Chapter Three
Economic Empowerment and the Village Revolution

1. In 1964, Ariyaratne wrote an article entitled, "The Target of Sarvodaya is Complete Socialism." In that article he said, "We should not

forget that there did exist a fully socialist Buddhist social system of this type in this country, and one inspired by Buddhism, as recently as eleven and a half centuries ago. . . . Sarvodaya workers are socialist in all respects." (*Sarvodaya Newspaper*, October 1964).

2. *Sarvodaya Strategic Plan for 1995–98*, (Moratuwa, Sri Lanka: Sarvodaya Press, August 1994), 12f.

3. A. T. Ariyaratne, "Transformation of Vision into Reality-Planning for Development (Awakening)," Speech delivered at the Asian Institute of Management, Manila, Philippines, September 1990 (Published by Sarvodaya Vishva Lekha Press), 10.

4. A. T. Ariyaratne, *Peace Making in Sri Lanka in the Buddhist Context*, (Ratmalana, Sri Lanka: Sarvodaya Vishva Lekha Press, 1987), 4.

5. "A Strategic Plan for Sarvodaya Members"(unpublished document), July 1994.

6. A. T. Ariyaratne, "Niwano Peace Prize Acceptance Speech" (December 1992), 25.

7. A. T. Ariyaratne, *The Power Pyramid and the Dharmic Cycle*.

8. M. K. Gandhi, (edited by A. Parel) *Hind Swaraj and Other Writings*, (New Delhi: Cambridge University Press, 1997; original essay written in 1946), 188.

9. A. T. Ariyaratne, *The Power Pyramid and the Dharmic Cycle*, 20.

10. While the book, *The Power Pyramid and the Dharmic Cycle*, made a good case for the need for a revolution, it seems probable that the book's outspoken criticism of the government and its policies also made the political leaders suspicious of Ariyaratne and his movement.

11. *Buddhist Thought in Sarvodaya Practice* (Ratmalana, Sri Lanka: Sarvodaya Vishva Lekha Press, 1995), 12.

12. Ibid., 11.

13. Gandhi in "Harijan," March 23, 1947. Cited in Detlef Kantowsky, *Sarvodaya: The Other Development*, 92.

14. Sir Charles Metcalfe, in a report in 1832 to the British House of Commons. Cited in Detlef Kantowsky, *Sarvodaya: The Other Development*, 87.

15. Karl Marx, "The British Rule in India," *New York Daily Tribune*, June 25, 1853. Cited in Detlef Kantowsky, *Sarvodaya: The Other Development*, 91.

16. *Sarvodaya: The Other Development*, 10.

17. Gandhi, a letter to Nehru, October 5, 1945, cited in *Hind Swaraj*, 149.

18. Detlef Kantowsky, *Sarvodaya: The Other Development*, 75.

19. A. T. Ariyaratne, *The Power Pyramid and the Dharmic Cycle*, 48, 53.

20. Ibid., 58.

21. Ibid., 97.

22. See *Mahāvaṃsa*, 1.84.

23. As Ananda Wickremeratne and others have pointed out, the idea of Sri Lanka as Dhammadīpa has been central to Sinhala Buddhist ideology and nationalism. Ananda Wickremeratne, *Buddhism and Ethnicity in Sri Lanka: A Historical Analysis* (Kandy, Sri Lanka: International Centre for Ethnic Studies and Vikas Publishing House Ltd., 1995), 86.

24. "Political Institutions and Traditional Morality," *Dana*, Vol. viv, No. 9 (Sept. 1989), 16.

25. *Dana*, Vol. xi, No. 3, 4.

26. Ibid.

27. N. Hennayake, "Ideological Impediments and the Role of Private Voluntary Organizations: The Case of Sarvodaya,"(unpublished paper, 1988), 26.

28. Richard Gombrich and Gananath Obeyesekere, *Buddhism Transformed: Religious Change in Sri Lanka*, 250.

29. Ibid., 252.

30. Quotes from Marx, *Op. Cit.*, 91

31. Richard Gombrich and Gananath Obeyesekere, *Buddhism Transformed*, 251–252.

32. *Op. Cit.*, 25.

33. Hennayake charges that Ariyaratne's use of the nationalist myth about ancient, spiritual Sri Lanka being a self-sufficient country shows his alignment with "the ruling elite groups [who] have never given up this indigenous discourse on popular history as a form of legitimation. . . ." Hennayake also charges that the Sarvodaya Movement is based on Protestant Buddhist ideals and is "uncritically dependent on a myth of a glorious past." Ibid., 24.

34. "The Greatest Tribute to Mahatma Gandhi is Building a Sarvodaya Society in the Twenty First Century," (speech) New Delhi, September 1996.

35. A. T. Ariyaratne, *The Power Pyramid and the Dharmic Cycle*, 97.

36. See Sarvodaya's chart comparing these two systems in *The Power Pyramid and the Dharmic Cycle*, 128.

37. A. T. Ariyaratne, *The Power Pyramid and the Dharmic Cycle*, 91.

38. R. Pieris, cited in Hans Wismeijer, *Diversity and Harmony* (A privately published dissertation from the Department of Cultural Anthropology, University of Utrecht, Netherlands, 1981), 51.

39. A. T. Ariyaratne, "Gandhi Peace Prize Acceptance Speech, January 1, 1997, 14.

40. A. T. Ariyaratne, "Transformation of Vision into Reality-Planning for Development (Awakening)," 10.

41. Ibid., 12.

42. Detlef Kantowsky, "Gandhi—Coming Back from West to East?," from *Learning How to Live in Peace*, 28.

43. The members of the donor consortium were NOVIB, CIDA, NORAD, ITDG, and HELVETAS.

44. A. T. Ariyaratne, *Future Directions of Sarvodaya* (Ratmalana, Sri Lanka: Sarvodaya Vishva Lekha Press, 1994), 10.

45. Ibid., 16.

46. Ibid., 12.

47. A. T. Ariyaratne, *Future Directions of Sarvodaya*, 18.

48. Ariyaratne has discussed this incident in *Future Directions of Sarvodaya*, 16.

49. United Nations Development Program, *Human Development Report* (New York: United Nations Publications, 1994), 4.

50. D. A. Perera, "Donor Influence on LJSSS Strategy." (Unpublished position paper circulated to Sarvodaya leadership and others, 1992), 5.

51. Comments made in a meeting in Moratuwa, Sri Lanka in August, 1994.

52. Simon Zadek and S. Szabo, *Valuing Organisation: The Case of Sarvodaya* (London: New Economics Foundation Monographs, 1994), 26.

53. Ibid.

54. "Sarvodaya Strategic Plan" 1995–98, 5.

55. D. A. Perera, "Donor Influence on LJSSS Strategy," 2.

56. Ibid.

57. Interview with A. T. Ariyaratne, Moratuwa, July 22, 1994.

58. "Twelfth Sarvodaya Monitoring and Evaluation Report," 1993, 51.

59. "Towards Peace, Right Livelihood and Community Self Governance: A five year comprehensive plan for the Sarvodaya Shramadana Movement, 2000–2005," January 2000, 110.

60. "Paper on the Graduation Process" (Sarvodaya document), December 1993.

61. D. A. Perera, "Donor Influence on LJSSS Strategy," 3.

62. "An Endowment Fund for the Sarvodaya Shramadana Movement of Sri Lanka," booklet published by Sarvodaya, November 1996, 6.

63. "Towards Peace, Right Livelihood and Community Self Governance: A five year comprehensive plan for the Sarvodaya Shramadana Movement, 2000–2005," January 2000, 21, 37.

64. Ibid., 19, 36.

65. Hans Wismeijer, *Diversity in Harmony*, 89.

66. A. T. Ariyaratne, *Schumacher Lectures on Buddhist Economics* (Ratmalana, Sri Lanka: Sarvodaya Vishva Lekha Press, 1999), 3.

67. In his Schumacher lectures (1999) Ariyaratne said, "I was one of those fortunate persons to have read *Small is Beautiful* in manuscript form and urged him to get it published." *Schumacher Lectures on Buddhist Economics*, 2.

68. E. F. Schumacher, *Small is Beautiful*, 47.

69. E. F. Schumacher, *Small is Beautiful*, cited in *Schumacher Lectures on Buddhist Economics*, 3.

70. Goulet, *Survival With Integrity: Sarvdodaya at the Crossroads*, 86.

71. "Political Institutions and Traditional Morality," *Dana*, Vol. xiv, No. 9, September 1989, 13.

72. A. T. Ariyaratne, *Future Directions of Sarvodaya*, 14.

73. "An Endowment Fund for Sarvodaya Shramadana Movement of Sri Lanka," (Sarvodaya document, 1966), 8.

74. "Sarvodaya Strategic Plan" 1995–98, 8.

75. A. T. Ariyaratne, "Transformation of Vision into Reality-Planning for Development (Awakening)," 17.

76. Jude Fernando, *A Political Economy Of Nongovernmental Organizations In Bangladesh And Sri Lanka*. (Unpublished dissertation, University of Pennsylvania, 1998), 378.

77. Sarvodaya Shramadana Sangamaya, *Annual Report 1996-97*, 18.

78. Comments made in an interview with Saliyah Ranasinghe, Executive Director of SEEDS. (Ratmalana, Sri Lanka, October 17, 1997.)

79. "Sarvodaya Strategic Plan" 1991–94, 8.

80. SEEDS Annual Report, 2000–01, 26.

81. SEEDS, "Quarterly Progress Report, 1998," 2. The percentages of these loans were: cultivation, 14.6%; trade, 49.6%; small industry, 14%; services, 5%; livestock, 8%; and other, 8%.

82. With my research assistant, I visited twenty-one Sarvodaya villages during 1997 and interviewed people involved with the Movement. While this may not have constituted a complete cross section of the population, it did represent a good sample of the kinds of villages in which Sarvodaya is conducting programs.

83. Jude Fernando writes, "Not a single SSM *samiti* [village society] commanded more than 5% of the total population in a given gramasevake unit . . ." *A Political Economy of Nongovernmental Organizations in Bangladesh and Sri Lanka*, 378.

84. "Sarvodaya Annual Report" 1996–97, 18.

85. Comments made in village field interview, August 14, 1997.

86. Interview with Saliyah Ranasinghe, Ratmalana, Sri Lanka, July 31, 1997.

87. M. K. Gandhi, "Constructive Programme: Its Meaning and Place,"(1941) in *Hind Swaraj*, ed. A. J. Parel (Cambridge University Press, 1997), 170.

88. Detlef Kantowsky, *Sarvodaya: The Other Development*, 8.

89. "Experiencing Peace While Engaging In Experiments Based On Moral Principles." (Speech delivered in New Delhi, November 1996), 7.

90. *Application Of The Concept Of Right Livelihood For A Full Engagement Society* (Ratmalana, Sri Lanka: Sarvodaya Press, 1996), 4.

91. Detlef Kantowsky, *Sarvodaya: The Other Development*, 8.

92. A. T. Ariyaratne, *Politics, Politicians and Sustenance of a Contented Civil Society* (Ratmalana, Sri Lanka: Sarvodaya Press, 1996), 7.

93. A. T. Ariyaratne, *Schumacher Lectures on Buddhist Economics*, 44.

94. A. T. Ariyaratne, *Sarvodaya and the Economy* (Ratmalana, Sri Lanka: Sarvodaya Press, 1988), 11.

Chapter Four
Sarvodaya and the Political Empowerment of the Village

*Portions of this chapter come from Bond, George D.,"Conflicts of Identity and Interpretation in Buddhism: The Clash Between the Sarvodaya Shramadana Movement and the Government of President Premadasa," in Tessa J. Bartholomeusz and Chandra R. De Silva (eds.), *Buddhist Fundamentalism and Minority Identities in Sri Lanka* (Albany: State University of New York Press, 1998) 36–52.

1. Cited in Hans Wismeijer, *Diversity in Harmony*, 40.

2. "Words Together with Action," *Sarvodaya Newspaper*, April 1961. Cited in A. T. Ariyaratne, *The Power Pyramid and the Dharmic Cycle*, 31.

3. *Sarvodaya Shramadana, The Growth of a People's Movement* (Sarvodaya booklet, 1974), 38.

4. A. T. Ariyaratne, cited in Joanna Macy, *Dharma and Development*, 14.

5. A. T. Ariyaratne, *Struggle to Awaken* (Moratuwa: Sarvodaya Press, 1978), 19.

6. Detlef Kantowsky, *Sarvodaya: The Other Development*, 75.

7. Denis Goulet, *Survival with Integrity: Sarvodaya at the Crossroads*, 12.

8. Detlef Kantowsky, *Sarvodaya: The Other Development*, 75.

9. A. T. Ariyaratne, *The Power Pyramid and the Dharmic Cycle*, 59.

10. A. T. Ariyaratne, "Political Institutions and Traditional Morality," in *Collected Works*, Vol. V (Ratmalana, Sri Lanka: Sarvodaya Vishva Lekha Press, 1991), 63.

11. Denis Goulet, *Survival with Integrity, Sarvodaya at the Crossroads* 14.

12. Hans Wismeijer, *Diversity in Harmony*, 41.

13. Detlef Kantowsky, *Sarvodaya: The Other Development*, 64.

14. Cited in Steven Kemper, *The Presence of the Past: Chronicles, Politics, and Culture in Sinhala Life* (Ithaca, NY: Cornell University Press, 1991), 174. Jayawardene also said he had a responsibility to assist other religions as well.

15. Cited in Detlef Kantowsky, *Sarvodaya: The Other Development*, 63.

16. Ibid.

17. "Sarvodaya Shramadana Movement: Towards a Global Experience from a Rural Experience." Speech given in April 1978. Published in Ariyaratne, *Collected Works,* Vol. II (Sarvodaya Research Institute, 1981) 76f.

18. Anonymous, *Ethos and Work Plan* (Utrecht, Netherlands: Van Boekhoven-Bosch, B. V., 1978), 10.

19. Detlef Kantowsky, *Sarvodaya: The Other Development,* 67.

20. *Sarvodaya and Development* (Moratuwa, Sri Lanka: Sarvodaya Press, 1980), 18.

21. A. T. Ariyaratne, *A Struggle to Awaken* (Moratuwa, Sri Lanka: Sarvodaya Press, 1982), 10.

22. Ibid., Chapter III.

23. Ibid., 19.

24. Ibid., 20.

25. Hans Wismeijer, *Diversity in Harmony,* 166f.

26. Detlef Kantowsky, *Sarvodaya: The Other Development,* 251.

27. Steven Kemper, *The Presence of the Past,* 178. Kemper writes, "Jayawardene's conception of Buddhism as a religion of individual responsibility had several consequences, justifying both his disinclination to make Buddhism the state religion and his desire to remove Buddhist monks from political life and secular vocations."

28. A. T. Ariyaratne, *In Search of Development,* 46.

29. Steven Kemper, *The Presence of the Past,* 169.

30. Denis Goulet, *Survival with Integrity: Sarvodaya at the Crossroads,* 13.

31. Detlef Kantowsky, *Sarvodaya: The Other Development,* 77.

32. *Atta,* January 30, 1984. Cited in Abeysekara, "The Saffron Army, Violence, Terror(ism): Buddhism, Identity and Difference in Sri Lanka," *Numen,* 48:16.

33. *Dinarasa,* May 15, 1986. Cited in Abeysekara, "The Saffron Army, Violence, Terror(ism): Buddhism, Identity and Difference in Sri Lanka," *Numen,* 48:16, 18.

34. *Dinarasa,* Sept. 9, 1987. Cited in Abeysekara, 24.

35. Abeysekara, "The Saffron Army, Violence, Terror(ism)," 30.

36. Rohan Gunaratna, *Sri Lanka, A Lost Revolution?: The Inside Story of the JVP* (Colombo: Institute of Fundamental Studies, 1990), 293.

37. A. T. Ariyaratne, *The Power Pyramid and the Dharmic Cycle,* 17.

38. *Peace Making in Sri Lanka in the Buddhist Context* (Sarvodaya Press, 1987), 2.

39. *The Power Pyramid and the Dharmic Cycle*, 28.

40. Ibid., 26.

41. Ibid., 19.

42. Ibid., 2.

43. Ibid., 21.

44. Ibid., 3f.

45. Ibid., 21.

46. Ibid., 4.

47. Speech by R. Premadasa, January 2, 1990 at the Malwatte Chapter of Siyam Nikaya, cited in Josine van der Horst, *Who is He and What Is He Doing? Religious Rhetoric and Performances in Sri Lanka During R. Premadasa's Presidency (1989–1993)* (Amsterdam: VU University Press, 1995), 107.

48. Ibid., 131.

49. Ibid., 106.

50. Ibid., 131.

51. Ibid.

52. Stanley J. Tambiah, *Buddhism Betrayed?: Religion, Politics and Violence in Sri Lanka* (Chicago: University of Chicago Press, 1992), 92.

53. Johan Galtung, quoted in an interview by Jehan Perera in *The Island*, September 15, 1992.

54. *Sunday Observer*, April 28, 1991.

55. *Sunday Observer*, April 28, 1991.

56. *Sunday Observer*, January 12, 1992.

57. These summaries of his speeches are based on my field notes taken during travels with him to rallies during June and July, 1992.

58. *Daily News*, July 21, 1992. Probably because Sarvodaya was attacking the government for environmental pollution, many stories published in government papers during this period also tried to accuse Sarvodaya of polluting in various ways. Some stories argued that the Sarvodaya headquarters complex polluted its neighborhood in Moratuwa.

59. *Daily News*, July 23, 1992.

60. H. L. Seneviratne, *The Work of Kings: The New Buddhism in Sri Lanka*. (Chicago, Ill.: University of Chicago Press, 1999), 250–276.

61. The Siyam Nikaya is the oldest of the branches or "fraternities" of the Sangha in Sri Lanka. It has two divisions: the Asgiriya and the Malvatta. The other main branches of the Sangha are the Amarapura Nikaya and the Ramañña Nikāya.

62. Ibid., 258.

63. Ibid., 259.

64. Ibid., 264.

65. From Ariyaratne's speech to Dhamma School teachers in Hambantota, Sri Lanka, August 8, 1992.

66. *Sunday Observer*, February 2, 1992.

67. A. T. Ariyaratne, "This is Sarvodaya Politics—hereon we stand," *Sunday Times*, January 12, 1992.

68. *Daily News*, December 30, 1992.

69. Mahatma Gandhi, cited by A. T. Ariyaratne, "The Greatest Tribute to Mahatma Gandhi is Building a Sarvodaya Society in the 21st Century" (speech), New Delhi, 1996.

70. "Sarvodaya Policy and Strategy 1995–2001," (Sarvodaya document), Chapter 3.

71. A. T. Ariyaratne, *The Power Pyramid and the Dharmic Cycle*, 18.

72. "Politics, Politicians and Sustenance of a Contented Civil Society," (Speech given in Trivandrum, India, November 1996; Printed by Sarvodaya Vishva Lekha Press, 1996), 7.

73. A. T. Ariyaratne, *The Power Pyramid and the Dharmic Cycle*, 19.

74. Ibid., 99. Ariyaratne recognizes that the urban areas are also important and later spells out how they can be divided into groups of 250 families that function like village communities within the urban areas. (See "An Endowment Fund for SSM," Sarvodaya document November, 1996, 2.)

75. *Island*, June 22, 1986.

76. *The Observer*, March 29, 1992. Front-page story.

77. A. T. Ariyaratne, *The Power Pyramid and the Dharmic Cycle*, 178f.

78. This occurred during a speech at the Moor's Islamic Cultural Home in Colombo on May 21, 1997.

79. Sallie B. King, "Conclusion: Buddhist Social Activism," from Sallie King and Christopher Queen (eds.), *Engaged Buddhism: Buddhist Liberation Movements in Asia*, 430.

80. A. T. Ariyaratne, *The Power Pyramid and the Dharmic Cycle*, 117ff.

81. "Sarvodaya Strategic Plan" 1995–98 (Sarvodaya document), 19.

82. Speech to the Central Bank, Colombo, July 20, 1994.

83. Speech to Moors Islamic Cultural Home, Colombo, May 21, 1997.

84. Charles F. Keyes, "Millennialism, Theravada Buddhism and Thai Society," *Journal of Asian Studies*, Vol. XXXVI, No. 2 (February 1977), 297.

85. Keyes, "Millennialism, Theravada Buddhism and Thai Society," 302.

86. Keyes, "Millennialism, Theravada Buddhism and Thai Society," 289, 302. See also: M. Adas, *Prophets of Rebellion: Millenarian Protest Movements against the European Colonial Order* (Chapel Hill, NC: The University of North Carolina Press, 1979); and Aloysius Pieris, S. J., "Millenniarist Messianism in Buddhist History," *Dialogue* (n.s.), Vol. XXVII (2000), 15–25.

87. Steven Collins, *Nirvana and Other Buddhist Felicities* (Cambridge University Press, 1998), 413.

88. Sarvodaya's millennialism conforms to Keyes' observation that such movements "represent an ideological response formulated in the cultural terms with which that population is most familiar." Keyes, Op. Cit., 302.

89. Richard Gombrich and Gananath Obeyesekere, *Buddhism Transformed: Religious Change in Sri Lanka*, 203; also George Bond, *The Buddhist Revival in Sri Lanka* (Columbia, SC: University of South Carolina Press, 1988), 77.

90. Hansen observes that these movements represented ways of "responding to social unrest that conveyed a longing for the restoration of idealized conceptions of meaning and order. Even if these conceptions had never existed as historical realities, there was a perception that in the past, there had been a better more righteous world that could serve as a model for the future." Anne Hansen, "Ways of the World: Moral Discernment and Narrative Ethics in a Cambodian Buddhist Text," (unpublished dissertation, Harvard University, 1999), 26.

91. "Sarvodaya Strategic Plan" 1995–98 (Sarvodaya document), 19.

Chapter Five
The Road Ahead: Deshodaya, National Awakening

1. Denis Goulet, *Survival with Integrity: Sarvodaya At The Crossroads*.

2. "Towards Peace, Right Livelihood and Community Self-Governance: A Five Year Comprehensive Plan for the Sarvodaya Shramadana Movement, 2000–2005" (Moratuwa, Sri Lanka, January 2000), 12.

3. A. T. Ariyaratne, *A Buddhist Vision for the Future* (Moratuwa: Sarvodaya Vishva Lekha Press, 2002), 16.

4. Ibid., 11.

5. Vinya Ariyaratne, *The Sarvodaya Peace Action Plan* (Moratuwa: Sarvodaya Vishva Lekha Press, n.d.), 2.

6. "Towards Peace, Right Livelihood and Community Self-Governance: A *Five* Year Comprehensive Plan for the Sarvodaya Shramadana Movement, 2000–2005," 25.

7. A. T. Ariyaratne, "Five Lessons and a Goal," *Collected Works* Vol. IV (Moratuwa, Sri Lanka: 1989), 120.

8. A. T. Ariyaratne, *A Buddhist Vision for the Future* (Ratmalana, Sri Lanka: Sarvodaya Vishva Lekha Press, 2002), 5.

9. "Deshodaya" The Sarvodaya Initiative to Resolve the National Crisis" (Sarvodaya internal document), 2001.

10. *Daily News*, August 31, 1999.

11. *Island*, September 1, 1999.

12. A. T. Ariyaratne, *The Power Pyramid and the Dharmic Cycle*, 64.

13. "Towards Peace, Right Livelihood and Community Self-Governance: A Five Year Comprehensive Plan for the Sarvodaya Shramadana Movement, 2000–2005," 25.

14. The interviews discussed in this section were conducted in Moratuwa and Colombo during September and October 2002.

15. Abdullahi An-Na'im, "Religion and Global Civil Society: Inherent Incompatibility or Synergy and Interdependence?", in H. Anheier, M. Glasius, and M. Kaldorf, eds., *Global Civil Society Yearbook 2002* (Oxford: Oxford University Press, 2002), 60.

16. Vinya Ariyaratne, *Peace Action Plan,* (Ratmalana, Sri Lanka, Sarvodaya Vishva Lekha Press, 2001), 9.

17. A. T. Ariyaratne, *A Buddhist Vision for the Future*, 21.

18. Fr. Siri Oscar Abeyaratne. Article in *The Island*, September 25, 2002.

19. Michael Walzer, *Toward a Global Civil Society* (Oxford: Berghahn Books, 1995), 7.

20. Gordon White, "Civil Society and Governance" (Proceedings of a workshop by the Institute of Development Studies, University of Sussex, June, 1998), 379.

21. Abdullah An-Na'im, "Religion And Global Civil Society," 59.

22. This chart appears in many places in Sarvodaya literature. This version is from A. T. Ariyaratne, *The Vision of a New Society,* (Moratuwa, Sri Lanka: Sarvodaya Press, 1990), 7. For his summary of this chart, see Denis Goulet, *Survival with Integrity*, 11.

23. A. T. Ariyaratne, *A Buddhist Vision for the Future*, 11.

24. A. T. Ariyaratne, "Buddhist Thought in Sarvodaya Practice" (Paper presented at the Seventh International Seminar on Buddhism and Leadership for Peace, Hawaii, 1995). Printed by Sarvodaya Press, 12.

25. Joanna Macy, *Dharma and Development*, 42.

26. A. T. Ariyaratne, *A Buddhist Vision for the Future*, 14.

27. Joanna Macy, *Dharma and Development*, 46.

28. Ibid.

29. Comment made in a discussion with the author, September 21, 2002.

30. "SEEDS, A History of Development, 1987-1999,"(Sarvodaya Press, 1999), 16.

31. Ibid., 55.

32. Interview with the Director of SEEDS, Mr. Shakila Wijewardena. Moratuwa, October 16, 2002.

33. "Towards Peace, Right Livelihood and Community Self-Governance: A Five Year Plan for the Sarvodaya Shramadana Movement 2000–2005," 25.

34. David C. Korten, *People-Centered Development: Contributions Toward Theory and Planning Frameworks,* (West Hartford, CT: Kumarian Press, 1984), 301.

35. A. T. Ariyaratne, "Buddhist Thought in Sarvodaya Practice," 13.

36. "Towards Peace, Right Livelihood and Community Self-Governance: A Five Year Comprehensive Plan for the Sarvodaya Shramadana Movement, 2000–2005," 25.

37. A. T. Ariyaratne, *A Buddhist Vision for the Future*, 19.

38. A. T. Ariyaratne, letter to the editor submitted to several Sri Lanka newspapers in August 2002, but not published.

39. "Rules of Deshodaya, as adopted on October 2, 2001," (Ratmalana, Sri Lanka: Sarvodaya Vishva Lekha Press, 2001), 3f.

40. These interviews were conducted in Colombo in October 2002.

41. A. T. Ariyaratne, *A Buddhist Vision for the Future*, 16.

42. A. T. Ariyaratne made these comments at the annual meeting of the Deshodaya Organization in October 2002.

43. A. T. Ariyaratne, *A Buddhist Vision for the Future*, 20.

44. *Daily Mirror*, August 27, 2002.

Epilogue: Vishvodaya, World Awakening

1. David C. Korten, *The Post-Corporate World: Life After Capitalism* (San Francisco: Berrett-Koehler Publishers, and West Hartford, CT: Kumarian Press, Inc., 1998), 6.

2. David C. Korten, *When Corporations Rule the World*, 11.

3. Willis W. Harman, "Key Choices," in David C. Korten and Rudi Klauss (ed.), *People-Centered Development*, 10.

4. Alvin Toffler, "Third Wave Development: Gandhi with Satellites," in David C. Korten, ed., *People-Centered Development*, 21.

5. *The Post-Corporate World*, 21.

6. David C. Korten, "People-Centered Development: Toward a Framework," in David C. Korten and Rudi Klauss, eds., *People-Centered Development*, 300.

7. This conversation took place on October 17, 2002, in Vishva Nidetan.

8. David C. Korten, "People-Centered Development: Toward a Framework," in Korten and Klauss, eds., *People-Centered Development*, 309.

9. David C. Korten, *Post-Corporate World*, 241.

10. Ibid., 281.

11. David C. Korten, *When Corporations Rule the World*, 10.

12. On the idea of "utopia," see Steven Collins, who discusses two meanings of utopia: "utopias as descriptions of real (actual or possible) ideal societies or as acknowledged fictions which embody a critique of the writer's actual society." *Nirvana and Other Buddhist Felicities: Utopias of the Pali Imaginaire* (Cambridge: Cambridge University Press, 1998), 112.

13. M. K. Gandhi, *Hind Swaraj and Other Writings*, 150.

14. Sulak Sivaraksa, *Seeds of Peace* (Berkeley, CA: Parallax Press, 1992), 44.

GLOSSARY OF
PALI AND SANSKRIT TRANSLATIONS

ahiṃsā   Nonviolence

anagārika   Homeless one. Term used by Anagarika Dharmapala to indicate his new role.

anattā   Selflessness, literally "non-self."

atthacariyā   Useful conduct

bhikkhu   Buddhist monk

Bodhi pūjā   Bodhi tree veneration

brahma-vihāras   The Four Divine Abidings: mettā (loving kindness), karuṇā (compassion), muditā (sympathetic joy), and upekkhā (equanimity)

dāna   Generosity

dasa rāja dhammā   The Ten Royal Virtues

dassana   An insight, perception

Deshodaya   National awakening

Dharma   A very broad and important term with many meanings, including: righteousness, doctrine, teaching, nature, truth, and moral philosophy.

Dharmadīpa   Island of Dharma, Light of Dharma

dharmavijaya   Conquest by Dharma

dharmiṣṭha society   Society based on the principles of the Buddha's Dharma

diṭṭhi   A view or speculative opinion

dukkha   Suffering or unsatisfactoriness

gramadana   Sarvodaya's term for village or field-level workers.

141

gram swaraj   Village self-rule

gramodaya   Village awakening

janashakti   People's power

jhāna   Trance state, concentration

karuṇā   Compassion

khadi   Homespun cloth

Mahāvaṃsa   One of the Buddhist chronicles of Sri Lanka

mettā   Loving kindness

muditā   Sympathetic joy

Nagarodaya   Urban awakening

panchayat   Village council

paṭicca samuppāda   Dependent origination

peyyavajja   Kind speech

Ram Raj   The Kingdom of Rama or God

samācariya   Peaceful living with all beings

samādhi   The meditation of concentration or one-pointedness

samānattatā   Equanimity, impartiality

sangaha vatthūni   The four grounds of kindness

Santi Rājā   King of Peace

sāsana   Teaching, dispensation

sati   Mindfulness or awareness

satya   Truth

satyagraha   Peaceful demonstration, "truth-force"

shramadana   Gift of labor

swaraj   Self-rule, self-control

swashakti   Personal power

taṇhā   Desire

upekkhā   Equanimity

vishvodaya   World awakening

BIBLIOGRAPHY

Abeysekara, Ananda. *Colors of the Robe: Religion, Identity and Difference.* Columbia, SC: University of South Carolina Press, 2002.

———. "The Saffron Army, Violence, Terror(ism): Buddhism, Identity and Difference in Sri Lanka," *Numen,* 48:16.

Aitken, R. *The Mind of Clover: Essays in Zen Buddhist Ethics.* San Francisco: North Point Press, 1984.

Ariyaratne, A. T. *Bhava Tanha: An Autobiography,* Volume 1. Ratmalana, Sri Lanka: Sarvodaya Vishva Lekha Press, 2001.

———. *Buddhist Economics in Practice.* Salisbury, England: Sarvodaya Support Group, UK, 1999.

———. *Collected Works, Volumes I–VI,* 2nd ed. Ratmalana, Sri Lanka: Sarvodaya Vishva Lekha Press, 1999.

———. *In Search of Development.* Moratuwa, Sri Lanka: Sarvodaya Press, 1982.

———. *Schumacher Lectures on Buddhist Economics.* Ratmalana, Sri Lanka: Sarvodaya Vishva Lekha Press, 1999.

———. *Buddhist Thought in Sarvodaya Practice.* Ratmalana, Sri Lanka: Sarvodaya Vishva Lekha Press, 1995.

———. *The Power Pyramid and the Dharmic Cycle.* Ratmalana, Sri Lanka: Sarvodaya Vishva Lekha Press, 1988.

———. "Five Lessons and a Goal," in *Collected Works,* Vol. IV. Moratuwa, Sri Lanka: 1989, 120.

Aung San Suu Kyi. *Freedom from Fear & Other Writings,* rev. ed., London: Penguin Books, 1995.

Berger, Peter L. "Secularism in Retreat." *National Interest* 46 (Winter 1996/97), 1–18.

Bond, George D. *The Buddhist Revival in Sri Lanka.* Columbia, SC: University of South Carolina Press, 1988.

————. *The Word of the Buddha: The Tipitaka and Its Interpretation in Theravada Buddhism.* Colombo: M. D. Gunasena, 1982.

De Silva, C. R. *Sri Lanka, A History.* New Delhi: Vikas Publishing House, 1987.

Eppsteiner, Fred, ed. *The Path of Compassion: Writings on Socially Engaged Buddhism,* 2nd ed. Berkeley, CA: Parallax Press, 1988.

Galtung, Johan. *Buddhism: A Quest for Unity and Peace.* Ratmalana, Sri Lanka: Sarvodaya Book Publishing Services, 1993.

Gandhi, M. K. *Hind Swaraj and Other Writings,* edited by A. Parel. New Delhi: Cambridge University Press, 1997.

Glassman, B. and Fields, R. *Instructions to the Cook: A Zen Master's Lessons in Living a Life that Matters.* New York: Bell Tower, 1996.

Gombrich, Richard and Obeyesekere, Gananath. *Buddhism Transformed: Religious Change in Sri Lanka.* Princeton, NJ: Princeton University Press, 1988.

Gombrich, Richard. *Precept and Practice: Traditional Buddhism in the Rural Highlands of Sri Lanka.* Oxford: Clarendon Press, 1971.

Goulet, Denis. *Survival with Integrity: Sarvodaya at the Crossroads.* Colombo: Marga Institute, 1981.

Guruge, Ananda. *Return to Righteousness.* Colombo: Government Press, 1965.

Jones, Ken, *The Social Face of Buddhism.* London: Wisdom Publications, 1989.

Kantowsky, Detlef. "Gandhi—Coming Back from West to East?", in *Learning How to Live in Peace,* edited by Detlef Kantowsky. Ratmalana, Sri Lanka: Sarvodaya Vishva Lekha Press, n. d.

————. *Sarvodaya: The Other Development.* New Delhi: Vikas Publishing House, 1980.

Kaza, S. *The Attentive Heart: Conversations with Trees.* New York: Fawcett Columbine, 1993.

Kemper, Steven. *The Presence of the Past: Chronicles, Politics, and Culture in Sinhala Life.* Ithaca, NY: Cornell University Press, 1991.

King, Winston. *In the Hope of Nibbana.* LaSalle, Ill.: Open Court Press, 1964.

Kotler, Arnold. *Engaged Buddhist Reader.* Berkeley, CA: Parallax Press, 1996.

Korten, David C. and Klauss, Rudi, eds. *People-Centered Development: Contributions Toward Theory and Planning Frameworks.* West Hartford, CT: Kumarian Press, 1984.

————. *The Post-Corporate World: Life After Capitalism.* San Francisco: Berrett-Koehler Publishers and West Hartford, CT: Kumarian Press, 1999.

————. *When Corporations Rule the World.* West Hartford, CT: Kumarian Press, and San Francisco: Berrett-Koehler Publishers, 1995.

Kraft, Kenneth. *Inner Peace, World Peace: Essays on Buddhism and Nonviolence.* Albany, NY: State University of New York Press, 1992.

————. *The Wheel of Engaged Buddhism: A New Map of the Path.* New York: Weatherhill, 2000.

Liyanage, Gunadasa. *Revolution Under the Breadfruit Tree.* Ratmalana, Sri Lanka: Sarvodaya Vishva Lekha Press, 1988.

Lopez, Donald, ed. *Curators of the Buddha: The Study of Buddhism Under Colonialism.* Chicago: University of Chicago Press, 1995.

Macy, Joanna. *Despair and Personal Power in the Nuclear Age.* Philadelphia: New Society Publishers, 1983.

————. *Dharma and Development: Religion as Resource in the Sarvodaya Self-Help Movement.* West Hartford, CT: Kumarian Press, 1983.

————. "The Sound of Bombs Not Exploding," *Yes!* (Summer 2002), 51–58.

————. *World as Love, World as Self.* Berkeley, CA: Parallax Press, 1991.

Nhat Hanh, T. *Being Peace.* Berkeley, CA: Parallax Press, 1987.

————. *Interbeing: Fourteen Guidelines for Engaged Buddhism,* edited by Fred Eppsteiner. Berkeley, CA: Parallax Press, 1987.

————. *Peace Is Every Step.* New York: Bantam Books, 1991.

————. *Touching Peace.* Berkeley, CA: Parallax Press, 1992.

Prebish, Charles. *Luminous Passage: The Practice and Study of Buddhism in America.* Berkeley, CA: University of California Press, 1999.

Queen, Christopher; Prebish, Charles; and Keown, Damien, eds. *Action Dharma: New Studies in Engaged Buddhism.* London: Curzon, 2003.

Queen, Christopher S. and King, Sallie B., eds. *Engaged Buddhism: Buddhist Liberation Movements in Asia.* Albany, NY: State University of New York Press, 1996.

Queen, Christopher, ed. *Engaged Buddhism in the West.* Boston: Wisdom Publications, 2000.

Rahula, W. *The Heritage of the Bhikkhu: A Short History of the Bhikkhu in Educational, Cultural, and Political Life.* New York: Grove Press, 1974.

Ratnapala, Nandasena. *Sarvodaya in Sri Lanka*. Moratuwa: Sarvodaya Publications, 1978.

———. *Study Service in the Sarvodaya Shramadana Movement in Sri Lanka 1958–1976*. Colombo: Sarvodaya Research Center, 1976.

Seneviratne, H. L. *The Work of Kings: The New Buddhism in Sri Lanka*. Chicago: University of Chicago Press, 1999.

Sivaraksa, Sulak. *Loyalty Demands Dissent: Autobiography of an Engaged Buddhist*. Berkeley, CA: Parallax Press, 1998.

———. *Seeds of Peace*. Berkeley, CA: Parallax Press, 1991.

———. *A Socially Engaged Buddhism*. Bangkok: Thai Inter-Religious Commission for Development, 1988.

Sizemore, Russell F. and Swearer, Donald K., eds. *Ethics, Wealth, and Salvation: A Study in Buddhist Social Ethics*. Columbia, SC: University of South Carolina Press, 1990.

Van der Horst, Josine. *"Who is He, What is He Doing": Religious Rhetoric and Performances in Sri Lanka during R. Premadasa's Presidency (1989–1993)*. Amsterdam: VU University Press, 1995.

Weber , Max. *The Religion of India*. Translated by H. Gerth and D. Martindale. NY: The Free Press, 1958.

Wickremeratne, Ananda. *Buddhism and Ethnicity in Sri Lanka: A Historical Analysis*. Kandy, Sri Lanka: International Centre for Ethnic Studies and Vikas Publishing House Ltd., 1995.

Wismeijer, Hans. *Diversity in Harmony*. Privately published dissertation from the Department of Cultural Anthropology, University of Utrecht, Netherlands, 1981.

Zadek, Simon and Szabo, S. *Valuing Organisation: The Case of Sarvodaya*. London: New Economics Foundation Monographs, 1994.

INDEX

Asokan ideals of, 74, 79, 80–81,
112
Buddhism in, 70–75, 79–81
Gandhi's views of, 46, 70, 71, 88,
112–13
LTTE settlement with, 36–37, 40,
76–77
open economics policies of,
43–44, 50, 61, 92, 93
peace planning with, 31
peace prizes established by, 37
Sarvodaya's severance from,
44–45, 50–53, 76–87
Sarvodaya's relations with, 5–6,
27–28, 31, 69–92
Sri Lanka, India, uprising against,
125n1
Ten Royal Virtues of, 72, 112
village, 87–89
violence caused by, 27–28, 30,
77–78
gram swaraj
banking for, 108–9
defined, 104, 141
deshodaya and, 113
Five Rs program for, 110
Five Stage Village Graduation
Model and, 107
meditation for, 108
Nagarodaya Center for, 110
peace by, 108
preparation for, 107–8
preschools for, 108
Right Livelihood society by, 66,
108
SEEDS and, 108–9
Sinhala village and, 45–46
technological empowerment for,
109–10
Urban Awakening Program for,
110
village development by, 107–8
gramadana, 141
Gramodaya Centers, 23, 142
grassroots organizations
against capitalism, xi–xii
developing, 21
for education, 68
for peace, 40

Gunaratna, Rohan, 77

Hansen, Anne, 92, *137n90*
Harman, Willis, 116–17
health care, 22
Helvetas organization, 24
Hennayake, N., 48, *129n33*
Hinduism
Buddhism v., 100
revival of, 9
Sarvodaya viewed by, 100, 101
values of, 9–10
van der Horst, Josine, 79
Human Development Report (United
Nations), 54
Hundred Villages Development
Scheme
expansion of, 23
launching of, 21
organizations of, 22–23
social infrastructure for, 21–22
success of, 23

Immigration Department, Sarvodaya
questioned by, 82
India. *See* Sri Lanka, India
Indian Peace Keeping Force (IPKF),
liberation from, 77
Indo-Sri Lanka Peace Accord, 76
information technology. *See* IT
Intermediary Villages Plan, 58
IPKF. *See* Indian Peace Keeping Force
IT (information technology), 109–10

Jaffna, India, Sarvodaya establishment in, 37
janashakti (collective or people's
power), xi, 3, 30, 69, 107
Janatha Vimukti Peramuna (JVP)
activities of, 28, *125n2*
banning, 77
Premadasa's opposition to, 80
uprising of, 77
Jayawardene, J. R.
assassination attempts on, 77
Buddhist values of, 71–72, 74–75,
134n27
capitalistic approach of, 74–75
election of, 71

socialism
  Ariyaratne's view of, 43, 45,
    127–28n1
  Sarvodaya's goals for, 43–4,
    127–28n1
spirituality
  banking and, 65–66, 108–9
  deterioration of, 32
  ecumenical, 13–14, 29, 99–103
  Gandhian, 102–3
  power of, 29
  SEEDS and, 65–66, 108–9
Sri Lanka, India
  Anuradhapura period in, 46, 48,
    76–77
  Buddhism resurgence in, 1–2
  capitalism in, 16
  colonial period in, 2, 29–30, 33,
    91
  consumerism in, 43–44
  as Dhammadīpa, *129n23*
  Dharma upheld in, 47
  economy of, 33, 93
  government uprising in, 125n1
  independence of, 1, *90f*
  Kanatoluwa, 7–8
  kings of, ideals of, 79
  LTTE combat against, 76–77
  modernization of, 32–33
  peace plan for, 42
  shramadana camps in, xi, 7–8
  village-based society in, 46–48
  violence in, 29–30
stereotyping Buddhism, 1–2, 11
suffering
  act of, 15
  capitalism as cause of, 14, 49
  ending, 16
  origin of, 14, 15, 28
Sumangala, Inamaluve, 84–87
swashakti (personal power), 30, 107

Tambiah, Stanley, 81
Tamils
  link-up program for, 41
  rioting among, 30
  in Sarvodaya Shramadana Move-
    ment, 30–31
  separatist movement of, 72

tanhā (desire), 14
"The Target of Sarvodaya is Complete Socialism," *127–28n1*
technological empowerment, 109–10
Technological Empowerment Division, 61
Temple of the Tooth, 97–98
Ten Basic Human Needs, 17, 59,
  107–8
Ten Royal Virtues, 72, 112
Ten Thousand Villages Development
  Program
  introduction of, 55–56
  problems with, 56–57
  refining, 57–58
  success of, 58
terrorism, 34, 36, 76
Theravada Buddhism teachings, 18,
  28
"Third Wave" of Sarvodaya, 117
Toffler, Alvin, 117

United National Party (UNP)
  peace promises by, 40
  Sarvodaya's relations with, 71, 74
United Nations
  relief efforts of, 36
  Sarvodaya support from, 36, 54
Unto this Last (Ruskin), 2, 8
upekkhā (equanimity), 18, 19
Urban Awakening Program, 110
utopia, village-based society as 46,
  140n12

Vajjis, 112
village development
  Ariyaratne's decisions for, 58
  banking and, 62–68
  businesses in, 64
  categorizing, 58
  credit programs for, 62–64
  economic empowerment for, 56,
    59–68, 103–10
  five stage model for, 55–58
  funding for, 55
  government for, 87–89
  gram swaraj for, 107–9
  Hundred Village Scheme for,
    21–23

Intermediary Village for, 58
loans for, 63–64, 108–9, *132n81*
mother's groups for, 22, 56
Peripheral Village for, 58
Pioneering Village for, 58
political empowerment for, 69–92,
  103–10
preschool programs for, 22, 56
reduction in, 57
Right Livelihood society for,
  66–68
savings programs for, 62–64
SEEDS for, 60–68, 108–9
shramadana camps for, 21
social reform replaced by, 20–21
technological training for, 109–10
Ten Thousand Village Program
  for, 55–58
Village Link-Up Program, 41
village-based society
  Ariyaratne's support of, 46–50
  criticism of, 47–48, *129n33*
  greed solved in, 49
  implementation of, 50–53
  levels of, 48–50
  Marx's views of, 45, 47–48
  model of, 45–46
  mythological level of, 46, 47, 48
  Sarvodaya vision of, 46–50
  self-sufficiency of, 49
  in Sri Lanka, India, 46–48
  superiority of, 46–47
  utopian, 46, *140n12*
Vinoba Bhave, 2, 8–9, 13, 69, 88
violence. *See also* peace
  Ariyaratne's view of, 29–30
  against Buddhists, 76
  consciousness, poor, as source of,
    96f
  economics as source of, *96f*
  factors contributing to, *96f*
  Gandhi's view of, 27
  government acts of, 27–28, 30,
    77–78
  LTTE acts of, 76
  mind power v., 28
  peace marches against, 34–35
  power, misuse of, as source of, *96f*
  Premadasa's acts of, 80, 81, 83

protests against government,
  27–28
source of, 28
in Sri Lanka, India, 29–30
Vishva Niketan
  founding of, 38–39, 42
  purpose of, 96
vishvodaya (world awakening), 95,
  115–20
volunteers, Sarvodaya, 24

Walzer, Michael, 104
war. *See also* ethnic conflict from
  1983-1997
  factors contributing to, *96f*
  relief from, 35–36
Weber, Max, 2
Westernization. *See also* capitalism
  Ariyaratne's view of, 67
  consumerism and, 59–60
  economics and, 49, 67
  of Sarvodaya, 52–55
White, Gordon, 104
Wickremerante, Ananda, *129n23*
Wickremesinghe, Ranil, 40
Wismeijer, Hans, 59, 71, 73–74
women, self-expression by, 22–23
work ethics. *See* shramadana camps
World Bank
  education defined by, 68
  failure of, 50

Young Men's Buddhist Association,
  11
youth groups
  education for, 21–22
  peace goals of, 36

Zadek, Simon, 54

 Also from Kumarian Press...

International Development and NGOs

Confronting Globalization
Economic Integration and Popular Resistance in Mexico
Edited by Timothy A. Wise, Hilda Salazar and Laura Carlsen

Dharma and Development
Religion as Resource in the Sarvodaya Self-Help Movement
Joanna Macy

Going Global: Transforming Relief and Development NGOs
Marc Lindenberg and Coralie Bryant

Socially Engaged Spirituality
Essays in Honor of Sulak Sivaraska on His 70th Birthday
Edited by David W. Chappell

Southern Exposure
International Development and the Global South in the Twenty-First Century
Barbara P. Thomas-Slayter

Sustainable Livelihoods: Building on the Wealth of the Poor
Kristin Helmore and Naresh Singh

Conflict Resolution, Environment, Gender Studies, Globalization, International Development, Microfinance, Political Economy

Advocacy for Social Justice: A Global Action and Reflection Guide
David Cohen, Rosa de la Vega, Gabrielle Watson for Oxfam America and the Advocacy Institute

The Humanitarian Enterprise: Dilemmas and Discoveries
Larry Minear

Pathways Out of Poverty: Innovations in Microfinance for the Poorest Families
Edited by Sam Daley-Harris

Rethinking Tourism and Ecotravel: Second Edition
Deborah McLaren

War and Intervention: Issues for Contemporary Peace Operations
Michael V. Bhatia

Worlds Apart: Civil Society and the Battle for Ethical Globalization
John D. Clark

Visit Kumarian Press at **www.kpbooks.com** or
call **toll-free 800.289.2664** for a complete catalog.